How to neurotypicals

A field survival guide for the neurodivergent

Abel Abelson

"THERE IS NO SUCH THING AS A 'NEUROTYPICAL'.
EVERYONE IS COMPLETELY AND TOTALLY UNIQUE – JUST
LIKE EVERY CAN OF COCA-COLA IS."

– ABEL ABELSON

DEDICATION

To all the weird, funky
and fabulous neurodivergents
in the Multiverse!

Rock on!

CONTENTS

PREFACE

Neurotypicals. Every morning, they rise from their graves like zombies, in massive swarms of barely conscious bodies. Numb and indifferent to everything but their own insatiable hunger, they mindlessly bump into each other - and into you. Drooling and moaning from behind their badly constructed masks of civilization and fake smiles, they corner and poke you. You can't reason with them. You can't explain anything to them that matters, because they can't understand. They don't care; instead, they crave. More. And then more. And then even more.

You, neurodivergent, have an especially succulent brain. They don't like your company, but they do like to suck you dry. Work for them, think for them, forego your nights and lunch breaks in service to them, they'll love it! They'll never love you, but they love munching on you. Every night, you regrow the parts of yourself they've feasted upon. Every morning, anew, they rise and, if they get a chance, eat you alive.

Well, it needn't continue like that. While it's true that they can't understand you, nor much of anything else for that matter, you can understand them. I know, they're not the most appetizing of subject matters. But either you learn what makes them tick and how exactly the goo in their skulls sloshes around, so you can predict their behavior, direct their attention, and make good use of their quirks and desires. Or you remain the victim of their insatiable, egotistic, and materialistic existence.

If you're into empowering yourselves amidst the mindless hordes, then put on your zoologist's cap now and join me in a fun and enlightening expedition into *Homo neurotipicus* territory. The risk is zero. The potential benefits are enormous: a new life where *you*'re in control because of your intelligence and knowledge, instead of *them* because of their sheer numbers.

Let's get to it!

WHAT YOU CAN EXPECT FROM THIS BOOK

This book is all about handling neurotypicals better. It aims to improve life – for them, but also, and especially, for us neurodivergents (or neuro*a*typicals if you prefer).

Neurotypicals are everywhere, and they're awkward, just as awkward as they insist we are. They won't bother to get to know us better, or appreciate us. But if we get to know them better, like an anthropologist studying an exotic tribe, a biologist doing field research on a strange species, or an apprentice horse whisperer learning all about horses, our lives will become so much easier, so much more enjoyable, and so much more empowered. So, if you're not quite a total normie, if you're not 100% "typical," that's precisely what you can expect from this book: fun, and empowerment, both while you're reading, and in the years to come.

First off, we'll review our options. Is it really necessary to learn to handle them? Can't we just evade those pesky normies, ignore them, or escape? The answer is: yes, we can, but at considerable costs, and with great, specific difficulties to surmount. You'll see for yourself that handling them is

3

definitely a worthwhile option to consider. (And that's an understatement).

Then, before we dig into the specifics of *Homo neurotipicus*, we need to do a bit of digging in ourselves. All humans, but neurodivergents maybe even a bit more than others, make three huge, fundamental mistakes, which in turn make us unhappy, independently of our surroundings. As long as we don't correct these mistakes in our own minds, we could live in Paradise and still feel miserable. Once this Trio of Turmoil is eradicated, we can be happy in Hell, and all the more in this precious life. You'll learn what these three mistakes are, and how to overcome them.

Then it's time to get our hands dirty. Neurotypicals. *Homo neurotipicus*. What makes this awkwardly "normal" animal tick? How does their mind and brain fundamentally work, compared to ours? What are the bases of their social structures, which in turn give rise to these weird, seemingly illogical or even pestiferous behaviors? And more importantly: what can we do, or abstain from doing, to live a fulfilled, empowered, f*ing great life on this beautiful planet where they happen to abound?

Clear descriptions, marinated in a nice little sauce of soothing sarcasm (we can just as well have some fun in the process, right?), culminate in concrete, condensed rules for survival you can immediately apply in your life right now. You'll become another person after reading this. A wiser, happier, and empowered person, ready to make this planet your oyster again.

Finally, in a few afterthoughts, we briefly discuss the special cases of neurotypical parents and teachers. If anything or anyone can make life miserable on this planet, it's definitely them. But, as with everything, there's a lot of optimization we can do. If we go about it smartly, applying what we've learned earlier on in the book, we can decimate their obnoxious effects on our lives, and they won't even notice the difference.

We'll ultimately end our excursion in neurotypical territory with a crucial distinction we all have to learn to make: that between psychopaths and neurotypicals. The former disguise as the latter, but they're far more dangerous. The final pages of this book put you in the right direction to defend yourself from these predators, and to avoid making vital mistakes.

So, are you ready for some enlightenment, empowerment and a good dose of fun? Let's go!

HANDLE NEUROTYPICALS? EEEOOW! WHY NOT SIMPLY AVOID THEM?

Let's face it, neurotypicals are a f*ing pain in the butt. If you don't feel this way at least sometimes, you probably wouldn't have picked up this book in the first place.

To make things considerably worse, they're also omnipresent.

This leaves us neurodivergents with two options only: constantly avoid them, or learn to deal with them. This book is all about the second option: dealing with them. But before we get into that, let's explore the first option: avoidance. If that would work, why not? If I don't *have* to handle them, I *won't*. I'm not a masochist after all.

I'll be honest: I think avoiding strategies make life miserable, independently of whether they actually work or not (which I think they don't). Avoiding these omnipresent neurotypicals boils down to marking most of the physical, psychological and social space in this world "off limits" to yourself. This is in itself a good enough reason to avoid avoiding them.

But let's be thorough and go over the avoidance options anyway. Let's see if they actually hold some promise as practical solutions at all.

OFF THE GRID AND ON THE RUN!

NATURE HERMIT

The most obvious form of avoidance is, of course, physical avoidance. This can theoretically be realized in various ways. You can scout for a piece of uninhabited land far away from neurotypical 'civilization' (some prefer the word 'infestation'), and settle there for instance. Let's call this the 'nature hermit' approach. Alas, this isn't as easy as it may seem.

To start with, pieces of land that are both habitable *and* uninhabited, are extremely rare - no thanks to mindless population growth, rampant pollution and global warming, which coincidentally also seem to be the favorite pastimes of our neurotypical friends. There remains the active volcano crater here and there of course, if you fancy a nice warm climate all year round, or the quiet depths of the Mariana Trench (although even there the neurotypical's best friend, the plastic bag, has invaded the terrain). But all in all, we can safely say that there's not an abundance of *human-friendly* free space left on this planet, or elsewhere in the known Universe for that matter.

To make things worse, a piece of land that's habitable, uninhabited *and* that hasn't been claimed as someone's property already is probably non-existent. Even the seas and the Earth's poles have been carved into proprietary spaces. And if you *were* to find an unclaimed, uninhabited space and settle there, within very short notice you'd have to defend your existential right to be there, legally and/or physically, against quite a few others. Neurotypicals don't have a history of peacefully minding their own business and leaving everyone be - ask any indigenous population on Earth. Which brings us back to dealing with neurotypicals instead of avoiding them, and defeats our original purpose of avoidance altogether.

8

Bottom line: free pieces of land on Earth are very hard to find, and even harder to keep. Start building your rocket to the closest exoplanet (and make sure you're not being followed on the way there), or read on for other options.

URBAN HERMIT

You might try living at night in a big city, anonymously, in the street (otherwise you would have to pay rent or a loan and again deal with neurotypicals), scavenging half-toxic trash for food, clothes, and makeshift shelter. This is the 'urban hermit' approach. But apart from the fact that your health and general wellbeing would probably be in a deplorable state in no time, you would still have to deal with neurotypicals regularly, and from a very disadvantageous position. Vagabonds regularly get attacked and raped, and are harassed by police officers and upright citizens alike, whose hearts bleed compassionately for every ostentatious good cause you can imagine, except if it happens to reside on the sidewalk in front of their house in a smelly sleeping bag. Not a great solution either.

A small village is another option, but... Neurotypicals are really heavy on social control and in a small village everyone knows and checks everyone. In Mexico there's a saying: "Small village, big inferno", and it definitely applies not only to Mexican villages, nor to especially small ones. In a big city you can go unnoticed as a vagabond, disappearing in the anonymous crowds (who will occasionally treat you with a nice beating, robbery and even rape, I should add). But a village doesn't provide that kind of anonymity so you would attract quite some negative attention with your avoidant behavior. Being 'asocial' (and I'm not even talking about antisocial) is definitely one of the capital sins in the neurotypical book, so some kind of contemporary version of being burnt at the stake or chained to the pillory and serially spit at might just become the grand apotheosis of your village disappearing act.

9

STUCK IN THE MIDDLE WITH THEM

Well, the bad news is that however tiring, unpleasant, and even impossible it may seem to constantly deal with neurotypicals, it might very well be that constantly avoiding them is actually even worse.

For starters, and apart from the practical problems, it's giving in to them completely. That simply doesn't feel right. We have a duty, not only to our true selves but also to our fellow neurodivergents, young and old, to carve out and defend a space to live in *as we are*. Without seeking to crush others, but without letting us be crushed either. Endlessly scattering away like frightened mice the moment we spot a neurotypical approaching isn't a life. Not for us, not for the future generations. It's stressful, senseless and irresponsible.

Second of all, avoiding neurotypicals is practically impossible, just like avoiding flies or dust is. Neurotypicals are everywhere. And if there happens to be a place, a *sanctuary*, where they aren't already, you can bet your life that soon they'll be stumbling along, honking, making selfies and dumb jokes, and shoving each other and you around. Especially (but not even exclusively) if there's something, anything, to be gained for them. They're not evil incarnate (they're too ordinary for that), but they're not exactly the most considerate and delicate life form on Earth either, something most of them will gladly, and even proudly, acknowledge.

In short, planet Earth is a very crowded place and *Homo neurotipicus* is a quite invasive and mobbish species, so physical avoidance is not easily accomplished. If you do feel like trying, you might want to get a black belt in a few martial arts and a big knife for self-defense. And settle for very little sleep.

Or (recommended option) you might read on and check out what other possibilities lie in front of you.

THE OM OVERDOSE

Apart from physical avoidance, there's also mental avoidance. You can, in various ways, shield yourself and "disappear" mentally. Doing such a mental David Copperfield trick can be pulled off with the aid of legal or illegal drugs, or by mental or spiritual techniques.

Trying to constantly perceive or experience only an undividable 'Oneness' or 'Nothingness' for instance, does alleviate certain symptoms of freaking out. But they come at a considerable cost. This cost is known in some Buddhist traditions as getting lost in Emptiness (Ku). Yes, you're shielded and untouchable, a beatific smile chiseled on your face, contemplating Nothing, but you're also lost to others, the world and to yourself. Emptiness will be all there is, and there won't even be a 'you' to enjoy it. Don't get me wrong: I think experimenting with these mental states is very interesting and even beneficial in many ways. The problem is not the state, it's a possible escapist use of it. The healthiest human mind, in my opinion, lives in Nothingness/Oneness *and at the same time* in everyday mundane existence, like two viewpoints on the same reality, neither serving to escape the other - they simply complement each other.

There are variations on this mental shielding or avoiding, with other names according to the tradition they are inscribed in, but in the end they all boil down to the same fundamental strategy: if used wisely and in small enough doses, an expanding and completing of your mental world (but not a way of handling or avoiding neurotypicals); if employed unwisely, a mental suicide or evaporation.

Personal benefits and dangers aside, most of these practices, especially if they're not incorporated into a larger institutional frame like monkhood, also risk getting you gently, but without an opt-out checkmark, pushed into psychiatric therapy. If you're thinking: "Actually, why not, the psychiatric institution isn't crazier than the 'normal' world, and at least they'll leave me alone in my cubicle," think again. Psychiatric therapy isn't aimed at helping you *as* the neurodivergent you are, it's aimed at curing you *of* your neurodivergence. Which, even if this is something you wanted (which I hope you don't, please don't hate yourself up to that point), is doomed to fail just like you can't turn a bonobo into a chimpanzee without gravely harming its mental and probably physical health.

There are psychoactive substances out there that promise heaven (which by definition is void of neurotypicals) and during a while feel like it too, but they always end up either not working anymore, or using you instead of you using them. Both ways, they invariably destroy your physical and mental health in the process. In short, it works like this: at first you'll actually think for a while you're blissfully happy, independently of everything else. But then the effect wears off, and you awaken to harsh reality from this rosy dream feeling more miserable than before you started. So you take another dose just to feel better. This new dose either needs to be bigger than the previous one for the same effect (that's how the brain works), or you'll have to be content with less effect (which you won't). And ultimately it'll wear off again, leaving you even more miserable than last time getting sober. This experience then repeats itself in ever tightening circles of less and less bliss, and more and more misery, while your liver, kidneys, and other organs gradually deteriorate into a useless pulp. Not to mention your ever growing dependency on some parasitic pharmacists or other types of drug dealers, and the necessity to feed them *and* your growing addiction at the same time. For this one, I'd say: definitely don't even try.

OYSTER OR TRASH CAN, WHAT'S IT GONNA BE?

Avoidance, whether it's mental or physical, actually robs you of your freedom instead of delivering more of it. Avoiding nuisance on the one hand, and ceasing to meaningfully exist on the other hand, will blur into one miserable mess.

If you're willing to pay this price for what is ultimately a very crappy deal, feel free to do so and close this book now. In that case the world isn't your oyster, but your trash can for you to suffocate in. If you're anything like me however, you'll refuse to settle for a miserable life in the sewer, dodging neurotypical turds, just because you're neurologically different. In that case, *do* read on and let's find out together how the world can again be the splendid oyster it was always meant to be.

So you've decided to read on and see what other options lie before you, apart from endless avoidance and mental suicide. Good for you! You're in for *empowerment* instead of en-cower-ment. Congratulations on your courage and welcome to the party. We're going to have great fun together!

THE TRIO OF TURMOIL (THE THREE ROOT CAUSES OF YOUR UNHAPPINESS)

This book is about handling neurotypicals. It's a survival guide for the neurodivergent in a human world (by definition) predominantly populated by neurotypicals. And we'll get to the practical details of that very shortly.

But even more than about neurotypicals, this book is about our unhappiness as neurodivergents. And if we don't understand the root causes of this unhappiness of ours, we'll never be able to really do anything about it.

Unhappiness is never created by an external factor alone. It's always an interaction between this external factor *and* our own way of functioning. I'm not going into a cheap "glass half full, glass half empty" rant. I'm talking about a deeper psychological and neurological level.

Certain traits in you, in your brain and behavior, *lock into* certain characteristics of something outside you *in a certain way*, and *this specific relation* is what causes you to be unhappy. Not you, not the neurotypical in front of you, but the way your respective characteristics lock into each other.

In order to change this, you can try to change the external factor (which is very difficult), you can try to change yourself (which is arguably even more difficult), or ... you can look into the relation - which is as easy as opening your eyes to reality.

After decades of wading through my own happiness and unhappiness, and those of others, I discovered that all forms of unhappiness are rooted in the three fundamental mistakes described below. Actually, you could write them with a capital M, 'Mistakes'. Because they're big, they're bad, and they're extremely common. Which may sound scary, but it also means that correcting them is the opportunity of a lifetime: the chance to make a new start and completely change the ball game.

By eliminating these Type Zero Errors from our minds and lives, we lay the solid foundation to make the powerful, genuine, and lasting changes to our lives that we really need. If we omit to adequately tackle these Mistakes however, whatever we do to become happier and more empowered will be fruitless, because we'll be building a house on a swamp, or treating the leaves of a tree while there's still a disease in the roots.

So let's get to it and clean house - thoroughly.

ROOT CAUSE #1: THE PERCEPTION PARADOX

HYPERDALTONIANS

I could go into a very long, very metaphysical, and equally boring oration on how we, humans, just like every other life form, only perceive a tiny fraction of reality. Which would be better written as Reality, with a capital 'R', to distinguish it from plain, day-to-day reality with a lowercase 'r', if you 'see' what I mean (pun intended). The first, the sacrosanct one with the capital 'R', represents 'Ultimate Reality', which no life form consciously perceives and even less processes. The latter with the modest lowercase 'r' represents the heavily filtered, twisted and almost stripped bare dimension in which we butter our toasts and wipe our butts (and occasionally poke our finger through the paper too, *that* reality).

If you need more convincing of the basic and undeniable fact that we only discern a tiny fraction of reality (both with uppercase and lowercase 'r'), think of all the electromagnetic wave frequencies we are happily oblivious of. We only perceive a tiny spectrum of them because we only have two very limited electromagnetic wave sensors in the front of our head (we call them 'eyes' most of the time). They react to wavelengths somewhere between 380 and 740 nanometers only. Everything above or below, including man's best companions WiFi, microwaves, a lot of stuff only hardcore scientists talk about during their nerdy dinners, and then a lot more stuff even *they* haven't even started to conceive, is completely outside the scope of our perception, our existential dimension, our 'reality.' The same goes for air waves (aka sound), touch sensations, tastes, smells, and so on: we only perceive a very small fraction of them, compared to some other animals, and especially compared to what's out there in the complete spectrum. Other animals have different windows on 'Reality,' which makes their 'reality' significantly different from ours. But none have the complete package, if that would even be conceivable.

If you could at this very instant see all the electromagnetic waves around you, instead of just the tiny window from what we call red to violet, it'd be like an acid trip multiplied by a thousand. And that's just sight. Add to that all the sound waves, all the smells, etc, you'd become even more stark raving mad than you already are (proven by the fact you're still reading this).

Anyway. You get the point. We're like hyperdaltonian (aka color blind) little shrimps in a violent ocean of crazy movement all around, in and through us, most of which we are very happily very unaware of. Just like you can't really explain sight to those who are born blind, a life form with drastically other perception organs couldn't possibly explain the parts of Reality that we cannot biologically perceive, even if they tried. So, already in that sense, the world isn't what we think it is.

But this small metaphysical excursion is just the appetizer. Now for the main dish.

A MODEL OF THE UNIVERSE THE SIZE OF THE UNIVERSE

Yes, we're getting somewhere practical, bear with me a little longer.

So, in theory we perceive not all that much, but still a *lot* of light frequencies, a lot of sound waves, a lot of perceptions, tastes, smells, etc. We have the hardware, the sensors for it. All together it's only a small fraction of 'Reality' (as explained above), but still, it's a lot. It's reality, with a small 'r', everything around and in us for which we have sensors.

It turns out however that, for practical reasons we'll come to in a minute, we only *process* a tiny part of reality and lose most of the rest of it. In other words, of the tiny part of

Reality that we somehow perceive, we only consciously only retain another tiny part. It's like getting one percent *of one percent* of the original package, which is really close to nothing (one-ten-thousandth to be exact, in this example).

The first loss (Reality versus reality, explained earlier) is due to the biological limitations of our sensory organs. What's the second loss, in *processing*, due to?

I hope I'm not telling you anything new by pointing out that the human brain is incapable of processing every minute detail of everything that happens in our reality. In order to survive as living organisms, we need to act and react swiftly. We cannot wait to know every last single detail about every aspect of the tiger leaping onto us. We immediately reduce the real tiger to "aaargh! danger!" or maybe to something a bit more detailed (but not much), like "bad-ass lethal furry animal with big teeth and claws moving rapidly toward me, aaargh danger", and then run as if life depends on it. Because it actually does. People with brains who didn't have this healthy reaction and who instead remained contemplating every exact detail of the tiger's complex existence, including the color of every little strand of its hair, the smell of its left ear and the viscosity of its saliva, weren't very good at surviving. This in turn didn't make them very good at reproducing their genes, which in turn drove them quite quickly to extinction. Most of us modern humans have inherited the more successful genes that allow us to survive, but also push us into terrible reductions.

The point is: we obviously make gigantic abstractions all the time. We cram stuff together in broad categories and forget or never even think about the details that distinguish them. We base our actions on general principles, on quick, very rough judgments, and on instincts (many of them biologically ingrained). We reduce the literally infinite and ever-changing ocean of data around us, in its endlessly high resolution, to a tiny collection of bite-sized chunks, quickly tagging them with broad key concepts, and acting as if they weren't changing all the time (which actually they are), so that our tiny human brains can do *something* with it. Like escaping the tiger, preparing a sandwich, lying to our parents and the boss at work, and other life-saving and -sustaining stuff.

In short, we have a (very) reduced model of reality in our heads, which we take for reality itself. (And I'm not even talking about Reality here, see above. Just saying.) If we were to become aware of reality itself (not to mention Reality) in its entirety and in its every detail, our brains would melt and that would be the end of it.

So we're like avatars in a compressed, rather low-resolution, 3D virtual game, surrounded by other avatars, of other humans and animals, plants, substances, and objects. Nothing you know is really real.

You don't believe me, do you? Do the following experiment. Simply touch the tip of your index finger with the tip of your thumb, right now. Rub them gently together. Feel the tiny ridges, the temperature, how it is firm and soft at the same time. Listen to the sound of the rubbing. Become aware of every detail of every dimension of the existence of these two fingertips of yours. See how long it takes, notice how you can keep adding details, and still miss out on so much. And that's just two fingertips in an entire, constantly moving universe.

So what we perceive as 'reality' is actually more of a virtual world; but instead of some programmers creating this virtual world, it's our own brain doing so. (Yes, I know, it might be programmers too, and we might be pieces of code, but that's for another book.)

The only model of the Universe that has all of the details of the Universe in it, all of the data present without any abstraction or reduction, is the Universe itself. What's in our heads, our minds, is and always will be a reduction. And that's perfectly okay, as far as we're aware of that fact.

But for us neurodivergents, there's an extra twist to the

story.

WRONG AVATAR

Our small excursion above into 'Reality', 'reality' and then the even more reduced version that our brain produces for our conscience to enjoy (bring out the popcorn) may seem very Matrix-like. You're free to go all the way there and even further, but within the scope of this book I'm going to take a practical side turn here. What does this all mean for our everyday life and happiness as neurodivergents, and how can we leverage this understanding beneficially?

So let's get practical and delve into the fascinating subject of how this whole metaphysical and neurobiological process affects our day-to-day relations with other people, and specifically with neurotypicals - the little beast that's precisely under scrutiny here.

Just like we make models of everything else in our heads and interact with those, we also make models of other *people* in our heads, and interact with those, thinking we interact with the real person out there. In programming it's called a 'digital twin.' You take a real device out there, you reduce it to a few measurable characteristics of special interest, you store those as numbers in a digital environment and update them from time to time, and the rest of the code now interacts only with this digital twin instead of the real thing out there.

We do exactly the same with people.

And as we'll soon discover, we neurodivergents tend to make especially faulty models (or 'mental twins' if you like) of neurotypicals. That's a basic error, with far-reaching consequences not only on a personal level, but even on a planetary scale. You think I'm exaggerating, right, especially with the planetary stuff? Read on and you'll see that it's even an understatement.

We walk around *projecting,* upon everyone we meet, a

simplified and gravely mistaken version of themselves, contaminated with stuff we borrow from ourselves, from other people and from pure imagination. We then happily interact with our own movie projection, all the while thinking we're interacting with the real person. It's as if they're holding a blank cardboard cutout of a human silhouette in their hands, on which our mind casts the moving picture of our heavily reduced and often ludicrously mistaken ideas about them. They do the same with us, and together we end up basically playing a very bad version of the *Muppet Show* among us. (We also do this with animals, plants, and even objects, but let's focus on people for a moment.)

We do this not out of stupidity or malice, and certainly not because we choose to do so, but simply because we cannot possibly grasp the complete complexity of this person. To completely comprehend it by the way, we'd have to fathom the rest of the entire universe, of Reality itself, because everything is interdependent with everything else. We simply don't have the hardware for this, nor the time, since we have a lot of gaming, goofing around and binge-watching Netflix series to do too. So we are 'condemned', mutually, by nature, to interact with reductions, with projections on cardboard cut-outs, with puppets and avatars. The fact *that* we do this isn't the problem, it's simply a given, an unalterable basic aspect of the human condition. The problem is *how* we do it, and more importantly even, that we're *unaware* that we're doing it *while* we're doing it.

There's good news however. *How* exactly we project, and how *aware* or unaware of this we are, are variables we can tweak to a large extent - which is exactly the aim of this book.

Next up: why we, neurodivergents, are especially in a mess with this. *And* what we can do about it.

ME, MYSELF AND I (OR HOW WE CREATE OTHER PEOPLE IN OUR OWN IMAGE)

Whenever we meet someone, there are inevitably gaps, unknowns, blank spots in our knowledge about them. Most often, there will be more blank spots than data, especially if you consider how complex human beings are, and how mysterious they can be, even to themselves. Even close friends and partners have significant blanks, both to themselves and to us, so this applies even to them, although to a somewhat lesser degree of course.

To make interaction possible we preemptively fill in these gaps, on the spot, with whatever we have at hand. We don't just stand there, completely dumbfounded and empty-minded, waiting for data to slowly and steadily materialize, our jaws hanging and our eyes empty - even though technically speaking we actually should, since we have next to no information about this particular new appearance in our life. Instead, we make a ton of assumptions, on the spot, in the blink of an eye[1].

As raw material for these assumptions we (unconsciously) use two main sources: ourselves as a kind of basic template of 'a human being', and other people we somehow consider 'similar' to the person in question.

I think we can all agree that these are lousy starting points. But it's either that or nothing, so that's where we start anyway - and where things immediately start going awry, *especially* for neurodivergents, as we'll see in a minute.

Let's briefly go over the second source of fillers first, namely 'similar' other people. For starters, we automatically assume that if something mimics a human being close enough, then it's not a hi-tech android or a perfect hologram, but someone of flesh and blood. Yes, that *is* an assumption, or do you actually always check that by pinching them or by performing a small biopsy? I admit that it's a wacky thought, but it does go to show how little we really, actually *know*, and how much we assume. But also on a more down-to-Earth

22

level, we go with a ton of quite detailed assumptions based on broad categories like gender, skin color, body type, pitch of voice, posture, clothing style, whether they look like our grumpy grandfather or remind us of the friendly neighbour's dog, how they smell and move, whether they have an accent, or mayonnaise in the corner of their mouth, and so on. You can call these ideas prejudgments, common sense, prejudices, crap, intuition, whatever you like. You can be in favor or against them. But however you call them or feel about them, we unconsciously indulge in them all the time. Or when was the last time you took about a week of in-depth mutual getting to know each other in very profound ways before interacting with a stranger, a colleague at work, or maybe even your partner? And repeated this process at a regular basis to keep up with their ever-changing deep mental and physical states and evolutions in their busy lives?

So we definitely use our previous experiences with other, 'similar' people, and that's undeniably a very common and often unwise thing to do, but it's how we're wired. But that's not the part I'd like to develop here. What is of much more importance to us, neurodivergents, is the other source of fillers and how we use those: our own person. Because when we project our highly uncommon, fabulously neurodivergent self on a neurotypical, or even worse on a *society* of neurotypicals, we're typically so far off that it's almost like a psychosis.

We use our own person as a model for how others function, and we do this automatically, unconsciously, and very, very often. It underlies an astonishingly gigantic part of our ideas about the world, and other people in it. I call this 'self-projection:' projecting our own self-image, or the ideas we have about ourselves, on other people, believing they have the same characteristics we presume to have.

At times this process becomes more or less conscious. We may for instance think that since *we* wouldn't be capable of doing something, someone else wouldn't be either. Psychopaths and serial killers thrive on this: they look like us, they seem to behave like us, yet they genuinely revel in things that are utterly horrendous and disgusting to us. But since, caught in self-projection, we simply cannot fathom this to be true, they get away with it right under our very noses.

We assume that when someone is crying, they're sad, just like we're when we cry. Fakers and actors aside, this is true in most cases. But the *reasons why* they're sad may be extremely different from ours. For instance, narcissistic people may genuinely, heartrendingly cry because their overly inflated public image has been somewhat reduced to a more realistic version. A vengeful person may be genuinely sad because their vengeance failed. An extremely materialistic person may be genuinely in tears because they missed out on acquiring the latest must-have fad. As long as we're self-projecting, we assume however they're sad for a reason similar to what we'd be sad for, and we may even become accomplices to wrongdoings in the process.

The above are just a few of the more obvious examples of self-projection. In reality self-projection pervades most of our perceptions, interactions, and the mental models we have of other people - even of those we think we know quite well. It's hard to prove this black on white of course, but through careful observation of yourself and others you can start to detect self-projection going on all the time.

We all create our fellow human beings (partly) in our own, very personal image. This is already a problem when it happens between neurotypicals. But given that we, neurodivergents, by definition are different from neurotypicals in profound and radical ways, using ourselves as a base for understanding them and predicting their behavior gets us in big trouble.

I referred to the self-projecting mind as being almost in a state of psychosis, in the sense that there's a loss of contact with reality, or a grave distortion of reality going on. For neurotypicals this 'psychosis' is very mild or nonexistent, since the differences between themselves (a neurotypical) and most people around them (also neurotypicals), are small and superficial. For us, neurodivergents, however, the psychotic effect can be quite important - just as important as the difference between us and most (neurotypical) people surrounding us.

The practical results of this 'psychosis' can be hilarious (rarely), frustrating (often), or devastating (always *too* often). The devastation can be at our own expense, but also at the expense of the world around us. If we project, for instance, a higher degree of intelligence, consciousness, or empathy on the people around us than they really have, we'll entrust them with stuff they actually cannot handle in a safe or responsible way, and severe damage will ensue. Sad examples of this might range from traffic accidents and epidemics of civilization diseases like cancer, to global warming, large-scale species extinctions, and global environmental disasters.

RULES FOR SURVIVAL: DON'T LET YOUR SELF-PROJECTION MAKE A FOOL OUT OF YOU!

Rule #1: Remember: you're fabulously, but undeniably weird. Never assume that another person is 'basically' or 'fundamentally' the same as you. Better still, in *your* specific case (you being a neurodivergent) assume, to start with, that they *are* different *in every possible way*, and gradually find convergence points if there are any. That's a lot safer than assuming they're just like you, only to bump into brick walls and wreak havoc on yourself and your surroundings while you painfully and slowly realize how different they really are.

It takes a profound integration of the concept of neurodiversity, a good deal of practice, and a talent for concentration and awareness to be able to catch your projections as they unfold. This enables you to consciously counterbalance them. To make things even more challenging, most personality traits or neurobiological characteristics aren't binary (like in: either you have them or you don't). In reality everyone has most of them to a certain degree, and according to circumstances like exhaustion, sickness, emotional events, hangovers or even just noisy surroundings, the same person may have different degrees on different occasions. This means that even if someone displayed a certain amount of eg. empathy or intelligence under a certain circumstance, you can't just tick the checkmark. Instead you'll have to observe them over a longer period of time and in a variety of circumstances.

In any case, if you unconsciously presume others to be on the same spot on these scales as you, you'll regularly be in trouble, often in big trouble and occasionally in really, really knee-deep shit.

Take a margin of safety and start by assuming a big difference, then work your way, safe and sound, towards filling in the blanks with data and having a clearer picture of the person in question. At all times remain ready to question everything you thought you knew, however.

Rule #2: If it quacks like you and walks like you, it still may be very different from you. Never assume that someone who *behaves* like you, actually *is* like you. Talk is dirt cheap, we already know that, although we don't always act accordingly. But acts can be, too. Superficial behavior, like giving gifts or speaking nice words can come from drives as completely different as genuinely wanting the other person to feel good, pickup artistry, making someone feel indebted, and manipulating people for personal and even sadistic purposes. Don't let yourself be fooled by one-offs, or even a pattern in a certain situation. People have seen the person who was their perfect dating prince or princess turn almost instantaneously into a psychopathic monster after marriage, and there's a reason why there are sayings like "being stabbed in the back."

Rule #3: Never presume that someone who doesn't behave like you now, can or wants to *learn* to behave like you in the future. A secondary, but equally important and dangerous form of self-projection is projecting the ability to *learn* or evolve onto others. This form of self-projection is massively present among do-gooders and world improvers. They think that by ostentatiously giving the good example, people will simply follow suit and the face of the planet will change. *Some* people obviously do genuinely follow suit (most of whom are people who don't even need ostentatious examples but simply information). Others copy the behavior because it makes them look cool or morally superior. But most don't follow suit, because most people's (read: neurotypicals') brains don't have the same learning capacities as your neurodivergent brain has.

I'm not saying that showing your actions, informing and explaining is useless. It definitely needs to be done. But you should be aware of the fact that it'll only genuinely inspire a quite limited number of people (namely those with very similar brain characteristics as you), and even those only in a limited manner (it doesn't quite work like Ctrl-C Ctrl-V either). And the more neurodivergent you are, the smaller this number will be.

If you still think that you can change people in the direction of your choice, consider this. First of all, it's already extremely difficult for someone to change in a way that they *themselves* wholeheartedly desire - like eating less junk, doing more physical exercise, becoming more organized, or more outgoing. The myriads of failed New Year's resolutions convincingly prove this year after year. How much more improbable is it then that they'll change the way *you* desire them to change? Second, you aren't the only one wishing certain changes in a certain person. The person in question is subject to the desires and influence of countless other people, dead and alive, close by and far away: family, friends, colleagues, writers, Youtubers, marketing agencies, and creators of mindless internet memes and viral kitten videos all vie for their attention - and get it, too (especially the latter it seems). Your influence is just a drop in the ocean of all these other, often contradictory influences. Why then would they change exactly and exclusively in the way you desire? Seen like this, the chances that someone changes in a direction that you have in mind are extremely slim, and counting on such a change is asking for disappointment, or even worse, disaster.

Take people's current behavior as a given, not a variable, and try to create a change anyway if that's what you feel you should do. (Yes, I know that's a paradox, but I'm sure you can handle it.) Just don't *count* on it happening. If you succeed, hurray. If you don't, that's what you expected. You have at least remained on the safe side and no bones have been broken; and since you tried, your conscience is clear.

Rule #4: You're not alone. Never infer that absolutely no-one out there is like you. At times it may look like you're all alone being 'like you' and that there's no-one even remotely similar to you out there. While there's a minute chance that this is true (although you probably aren't all *that* special or weird that among the *billions* of people on Earth you are completely incompatible with *absolutely every* other individual), there are other possible explanations. You might have been so busy overadapting and mimicking neurotypical behavior, and the same may be true for those other people like you, that it has become almost impossible to mutually *recognize* each other as actually similar beings. You may have been together at the same party, both thoroughly hating every aspect of it, and both so successfully mimicking joy and integration, that you didn't even recognize each other's similarities.

The point is: if you don't show yourself as you truly are, ever, to no-one, by definition you, the *real* you, will always be lonely. If two people both living in a fortress never come out of the safe confines of their reinforced walls to even have a look at each other, they'll never meet each other and they'll die lonely and miserable while they could have had at least one good friend.

This doesn't mean of course that you should just show off your weird (from the viewpoint of neurotypicals, that is) self to everyone everywhere. You don't just throw open the doors of your fortress and let the whole world come and party inside, only to find yourself just as lonely again the next day, with the only difference that your complete interior has been destroyed, you trip over empty beer bottles, there's vomit under your bed and a turd in your sink, and you find cigarette butts for weeks to come in the weirdest places (end of metaphor, I think you get the picture). You can drop a hint now and then, vocally, visually or otherwise, for those of good understanding to catch. Be just that *little bit* weird that doesn't alarm neurotypicals too much (they're indifferent enough to not really notice). It will show potential 'others like you' that they might have some special compatibility with you. You can gradually let these select other people, the *maybe's* as you could call them, a bit further into your personal garden, step by step, so that if it goes wrong after all, they still didn't get very close. The damage will be manageable and you can easily recover. And you should consider the fact that no social damage is actually 'real'. It may hurt but it doesn't kill, so the benefit of finding a true friend definitely outweighs the risk of things going socially a bit awry.

ROOT CAUSE #2: THE MASK IN THE MIRROR

As I explained above, we generally haven't the foggiest idea what's happening around us. Or more precisely, we *only* have foggy ideas and next to no real contact.

We live our lives as if we're wearing a pair of Virtual Reality glasses on which our brain displays reductions, abstractions and filtered, distorted concoctions, based on extrapolations, projections, and self-projections. The more we (self-)project instead of observe, the more virtual this reality is. Welcome to reality: it's virtual.

In the same way that we create avatars of the people and things around us in this game we call 'Life' or 'My Conscious Experience,' we also create an avatar, or even several, of ourselves. We construct something like a first-person shooter or sim where we give our character a range of scores on abilities and weaknesses, and imagine it being equipped with certain attributes and characteristics, and lacking others. This imaginary character then interacts with the imaginary other characters in the game, using its (imaginary) characteristics with or against the (imaginary) characteristics of the other avatars. It's like a huge digital twin orgy played on a buggy console.

At the same time, in the real world outside our 'VR-glasses,' as real people we're having real-life interactions, that couple back to our virtual reality - but with distortions and reductions. As long as our virtual world and Self correspond largely with 'real' reality, there aren't too many surprises, negative or positive. But the further apart our virtual reality from 'real' reality, the bigger, and mostly the more negative, the surprises and unwanted effects.

We already talked before about how we construct simplified and partially mistaken models of others. We do the same with *ourselves*, only here the reasons are somewhat different. With others the main materials for constructing avatars are self-projection and the extrapolation of experiences with 'similar' people. We construct our self-image mainly on the basis of outside pressure and what we believe others think, or should think, of us.

Let's explore this last point a bit further and jump head first into our own dark, deep waters. Just like at the bottom of the Mariana Trench, where plastic candy wraps mingle with the most outlandish natural creatures, we'll find in our own shadowy depths surprisingly familiar stuff joyously twirling around among the surprisingly weird. The key word here is surprise, as you might have noticed, which means: you aren't who you think you are. By far.

(CLEARING THE) EDUCATIONAL FOG

We exist in the midst of an ocean of often conflicting expectations. Our parents ask of us to be strong and have a career he can brag about. They also want us to take care of the children, the curtains and the cobwebs. The kids need us to be as relaxed, cool, and fun as possible (or impossible). Our partner desires that we're responsible, trustworthy, fun, adventurous, strong, and empathetic, all at the same time, and that we regularly wash our socks (they're right about that one, by the way). The dog begs for walks and play time. Not to mention the neighbors who expect us to be like them, the mayor who compels us to be faithful voters, people on social media whose stupid selfies we're supposed to like (or else digital revenge is upon us), and even our goldfish who incessantly seeks something from us, but instantly forgot what it was.

From these expectations we distill not just one, but several ideal versions of ourselves: one for our parents (socially successful and interested in their tedious garble); another 'me' for our macho friends (tough, cynical, competitive, maybe making dumb jokes about women); and yet another variation for our feminine friends (definitely never making dumb jokes about women). Add to that an elegant and decent disguise for social and professional occasions; and still another 'me' that likes sex toys and getting drunk for our crazy party friends. And the list of masks or *personas* goes on and on.

Finally, in the midst of all this confusion, we unconsciously also construct one secret, 'real' Self, which we only unveil to one best friend or intimate partner at most.

You might think that this latter version is a quite correct one, truly corresponding with whom you really are. Well, it isn't. Unless you've done, and continue doing, the very thorough, painful and never ending job of truly and radically honestly getting to know yourself as you f*ing are *however that may be* (updated by the second or minute), your ideas about yourself are far from the truth.

We don't want to be who we actually are, and even don't want to know who we really are, for two main reasons. The first is that we're actually very much worse human beings than what we'd like to be. The second is that, at the same time, we're very much better human beings than what we'd like to be. The first is quite logical: we all like to think in certain aspects more of ourselves than what we really are, because that makes us feel good, and as mammals we're programmed to do as much of the latter as possible. The second may seem counter-intuitive, but let me explain.

Let's say that our parents rammed into our little heads, when we were small and easily won over by the promise of either candy or a spanking, that it's important to be empathetic. Maybe we returned from school, just having witnessed for the nth time some defenseless kid being brutally and sadistically bullied and traumatized for life by the same juvenile psychopath as always, and we emphatically made a case for removing this rampant psycho from school, or even the planet, in order to protect the good-hearted kids of this world. And perhaps our parents took this display of empathy (because that's what it was) for intolerance and hate-speech, scolded us for describing the psychopath as the psychopath he or she was, and made us believe two lies about ourselves: 1) that we're thoroughly non-empathetic monsters and 2) that if we do display an empathetic reaction later in life, it's only and uniquely thanks to their education, which counteracted our supposedly monstrous, non-empathetic nature.

Young children don't have the luxury of questioning the ideas their parents have about them. They don't have a second frame of reference besides that of their caregivers to compare with. Apart from that, they're constantly under a death threat: if the caregivers stop *caring* they can stop *giving care* too, which at worst (but not unrealistically) means death by starvation. So the end result is that kids, up to a certain age, simply gobble up whatever ideas about them that are shoved in front of them and incorporate them into the fabric of the self-image they're creating bit by bit.

Let me rephrase that: the end result is that *you*, and *I*, and everyone else, simply gobbled up whatever ideas were put in front of us, and we incorporated them into the fabric of our self-images. This also means that whoever, later in life, doesn't engage in the arduous and heroic task of reevaluating all their values and of holding every piece of their self-image in an unforgiving (or maybe just *forgiving*) light under the microscope, and this in a continuous manner for the rest of their lives, they'll actually never have the foggiest idea of whom they really are. They'll know what their educators constructed on top of their real nature, maybe. But they'll never know *themselves*.

Once you *really* get to know yourself, you'll probably find out that you're neither all that fabulous, nor all that monstrous. In the end you're a very okay guy or girl with certain characteristics that are as expected, others that are completely unexpected, and still others that are definitely weird but not necessarily problematic once you get to know *and accept*, or better even *welcome* them. You'll also discover that most people include you in their social circle not for whom you really *are* but only for your superficial persona.

Knowing yourself better will allow you to exchange your circle of fake friends for people that are simply and naturally much more compatible with the real you. People you can wholeheartedly call 'friends.'

Things will get simpler by getting to know yourself, but like in every heroic tale there's a price to pay (or garbage to get rid of, according to your viewpoint): those who *think* they like you now won't like you any longer once you coincide more with your natural Self - but quality over quantity, right? And being liked for someone you're *not* is in the end equal to being hated. Why cling to that anyway?

PLANET YOU

So there's a lot of educational and social stuff going on that drives the construction of this artificial first-person avatar that we naively take for our true self. But there's more, a lot more going on, and it may be even more powerful than what we've mentioned up to now. It's biology, baby!

We're planets, or organic spaceships (which is arguably the same), in and on ourselves. The microbiological life in and on us amounts easily to a kilo and a half of biomatter, and recent studies have estimated that 90% of cells in the human body are bacterial, fungal, or otherwise non-human[2]. They're living in and on us like on a planet, interacting with us, secreting substances that literally change our minds. We don't only have gut feelings, we have gut ideas and gut actions, too. (Do an internet search on "gut-brain axis" for the increasing scientific evidence of how our microbiome steers our thoughts and actions.)

Not only are we a planet inhabited and partly governed by other life forms, also most of what we consider to be 'us' (our own 'flesh and bones') is completely unknown to us. Silently (mostly anyway) and secretly, all this unknown matter and life continuously cooks up, breaks down, pumps around and transforms substances that define to an impressive extent our neurobiological characteristics, our personality traits, our 'free will' actions, our mood states, and even whether we enjoy dipping buttered toast in our coffee or not[3]. The genetic and epigenetic machinery, together with the rise and fall of hormone levels in our bodies, define to an astonishing extent who we are. This is biology on such a fundamental level that we have no control, no 'free will' in this domain. In other words, we have hardly any real control over who we are, how we feel, and how we act and react.

Here again, we may, for various reasons, prefer to discard actual facts and biological truths about ourselves instead of acknowledging them and incorporating them in our self-images.

It is difficult to give up the sense of agency that reassures us that 'we're in control'. We're not. Acknowledging that is like a leap of faith, and for this reason also fabulously liberating if and when we succeed.

On a more personal level, we may want to avoid accepting the overwhelming influence of biology on our personality and our 'choices' for emotional reasons. Maybe we desperately want to be manly and think of ourselves as manly, but actually we may be quite feminine simply because biology endowed us with low levels of (prenatal) testosterone, to give just one example. Being feminine is in no way inferior to being masculine, not for men either (in spite of what your local testosterone-laden goon squad may bark at the gym). But if your ideas (or are they *really* yours?) about femininity happen to be negative, this is a hard pill to swallow. However, once you have completely savored the bitter pill, swallowed and digested it, and found and accepted who and what you are, *whatever and whoever that may be*, there is the peace and power of being someone whose ideas and self-image coincide with reality. And those are priceless things to have.

Describing how and why we come to have such mistaken ideas about ourselves, about this maybe finally unknowable and ultimately even non-existent self of us, is stuff for a book on its own. What's far more important now, is undertaking the journey out of the delusion. It's a journey everyone makes for themselves, and everyone encounters other things, other reasons, other constellations on this private journey. It would be of little use to describe any individual findings, as they'd rather distract *you* from *your* truth, instead of helping you find it. What may be of help, is knowing that one tried and tested way of setting about this journey is through mindfulness and meditation. I don't pretend that it's the only way, nor the best way for you, but it's worth looking into if the adventure appeals to you. There's probably nothing more satisfying in a person's life than to look in the mirror, take off the mask, and finally meet the man or woman behind.

THE EMULATOR ERROR

A definite pitfall for neurodivergents is trying to be, or at least emulate, a neurotypical. I for one got completely lost in that. I also judged myself harshly for it later on, after I developed a bit more observational power and insight in myself and caught myself red-handed over and over trying to behave like a neurotypical again and again. But I think a bit more lenience and forgiveness is appropriate: life amidst the neurotypical pack is f*ing hard, and all of us neurodivergents end up with strategies to survive. You can't blame yourself for trying to survive in any way you did.

The thing is, when you're completely absorbed in this survival strategy of emulating a neurotypical, you're unaware of the fact that you're doing this. You're so focused on blending in and surviving that you actually take yourself for the person you're emulating. In reality, it's as if your 'embarrassing' real self is choking in a tub, with your false, neurotypical-emulating self doing its best to keep it underwater, and out of sight.

Your emulator part is always busy faking to be happily neurotypical, joking and having fun with your neurotypical 'friends.' From time to time your real self tries to free itself, spluttering and gasping for air, but the emulator quickly pushes it under again, laughing away to divert attention.

All of this happens mostly under the radar of your consciousness, so for all practical purposes you may consider yourself to be much more neurotypical than you actually are. You hide your neurodivergence just as much from yourself as you conceal it from others.

To make things worse, this is a vicious circle. The more you behave like a neurotypical and hide your true self, the more obnoxious you will become to people who are really like you, and the more you'll have to seek the company of neurotypicals who will demand more neurotypical behavior of you - or else exclude you. In the end you're continuously miserable because the rewards from your neurotypical 'friends' aren't for you (your real you), they're for your cardboard construction of a 'you.' And the real you will be choking every day a little more, which you do feel deep down, and it hurts like hell.

If all goes well, you touch rock bottom and find something there to change the game. It may be a book (maybe even this one), an encounter, a long forgotten thing someone said to you, a story, a song, or even a realization that sprung up seemingly from nowhere in your mind. You'll ditch the antics and get real. Because whichever way you turn it, your real you never dies until you do.

RULES FOR SURVIVAL: GET REAL WITH YOURSELF!

Rule #1: Do your dark tourism. Don't assume you know yourself until you've visited all of your moldy catacombs. (It'll probably take a lifetime, or even a tad longer.) It's easy to lull ourselves into thinking we've done all the work, gotten all the skeletons out of the closet and are open and pristine like the little house on the prairie after a spring cleaning. You aren't a saint, so there's bound to be some weird and underwordly parts to you. They're there to stay, and they're really great company if you respect and value them. A good little demon inside can come in handy anytime, and may even save your life. Without hell (etymologically speaking simply 'the concealed place', where you hide everything you don't want to see), what's the point or fun in heaven, right? Either you live with your weird and wacky parts on a daily basis, or you're avoiding to face reality in one way or another and condemning yourself to Eternal Fakeness.

Rule #2: Do your happy tourism. Don't assume you know yourself until you've visited all of your fantastic gardens. (It'll probably take a lifetime, or even a tad longer.) We don't only have catacombs with skeletons, we also have lush and exotic secret gardens. You are not the devil incarnate so there's bound to be quite some great and exciting parts to you, and some of them may not be known to you, or maybe you refuse to see them because you think that's immodest or not done. Look into the mirror in all honesty and see the bad and the ugly but also the good.

Rule #3: Be a dedicated tourist. Revisit your catacombs and gardens regularly. Better even: never leave them entirely, but simply abolish the boundaries between them and the rest of you.

Rule #4: Be the dragon that never sleeps. Always remain alert for when you're sliding into character. It's not wrong or bad to slide into a character once in a while and be a bit (or even very) fake. There are many valid reasons for doing so and it's not a crime, not to yourself nor to anybody else. In the world as it is, it's often a great strategy. Just make sure you know *that* you're doing it, and return to your real self in time before you get lost. (Some characters can be quite addictive or overly convenient.) A mindful and benevolent part of you should remain guard. Don't let this guarding become self-torture, or a kind of Eye of Sauron however. Be nice to yourself, all of yourself. Everything about you is there for a reason.

Rule #5: Minimize the faking. Fakeness begets fakeness. The more you fake, the less likely it becomes that something real is going to happen to you, and you'll miss out on wonderful stuff. If the situation doesn't allow you to be honest, real and direct, you can at least shut up instead of laughing with the hyena's. That way you won't make it completely impossible for someone like you to like you, and seek proximity.

Which takes us to the third and last root cause of our unhappiness: blaming others.

ROOT CAUSE #3: THE BLAME GAME

If you picked up this book, chances are you have some resentment against or frustration towards neurotypicals.

No, let me refrain that. Neurotypicals are unbearably obnoxious beetleheads, and you and I know it.

The question is, what do we do with these feelings of frustration and anger? Direct them outwards, where they invariably hit a brick wall and bounce back in our faces? Direct them inwards, towards ourselves, and let them consume us? Look the other way, act as if they don't exist, and let them consume us anyway? Repeat mantras all day long? A self-inflicted spiritual lobotomy anyone?

I offer a better idea: let's use those 'negative' feelings to empower ourselves.

Let me take the example of mosquitos. As such (at least in non-tropical countries) they're innocuous tiny animals that only prick lightly, only at night, with no lasting consequences. They're not really dangerous. They *are* annoying as hell when you're trying to sleep however. Given this reality, we can deploy two strategies: blame the mosquitos for our misery, or blame ourselves. (I know the latter sounds negative, but bear with me, it'll become empowering soon enough.)

If we blame the mosquitos, we actually unconsciously expect them, or some higher instance, God or Nature or our mommy or the Little Man in the Moon, to solve the problem. We judge the mosquitos guilty of irritating our lofty selves. We then loudly ventilate our judgment and accompanying irritation all day long and half of the night, as if we expect that they or this higher instance will hear our plea, acknowledge our noble-born rights to a duly dose of undisturbed sleep, and carry out justice swiftly. I don't know about you, but although I always wholeheartedly executed my part of the above steps, it never ended up in the mosquitos going away.

If we 'blame ourselves' however (see the quotation marks? that's because we're getting into *empowering* soon), it's a completely different game. "Oh, so I don't sleep well at night when there are mosquitos around? Let's take *them* as a given, and *me* as the variable. What am *I* doing wrong, where do I entertain false hopes or unrealistic ideas, and why don't I take things into my own hands?" Once you detect the problem from *that* side, namely *your own*, you stop being the plaything of those damned brainless mosquitos and immediately become the person in charge. (In this case, you install a mosquito net, and *voila*.) Things become fabulously more easy and manageable, and the most annoying and seemingly unsolvable problems tend to become simple quirks of less-than-optimal organization that you can solve or substantially improve easily (can you feel the *empowerment* coming?). Because on *your* side you have a lot more to say than on someone else's side. On *your* side, you have *power*. (There it is: empowerment.) On *their* side, you're the victim, a prop, or collateral damage.

Even if you can't do anything at all to alleviate your suffering (which is almost never the case), at least you're still the one in charge and you can carry it like the emancipated man or woman you are. Sometimes the only thing that needs to change is your point of view. There are people in prison who succeed in transforming the dreadful punishment into a life-changing, nourishing experience - because they decided so. Surely you and I can manage whatever comes our way then.

While I wouldn't be caught dead comparing neurotypicals to annoying and somewhat dumb mosquitos (wink), the process with them is the same. As long as we whine and complain about them, instead of moving on to 'blaming ourselves' (read: empowering ourselves), nothing is going to happen, apart from us becoming a bit more bitter and unhappy every day. Once we position the problem on our side however, instantaneously we become the empowered party and there's a very bright light shining at the end of the tunnel.

There's one big hurdle to take, however, like in all good stories. You have to learn to see 'them' (whoever 'they' are) as a given and you as the variable, instead of the usual other way around. This not only implies a major paradigm shift, but it also needs you to mourn your rosy psychotic dream of all of 'them' becoming nice people. Mourning comes with denial, anger and deep sadness before acceptance and a new and better life. If you've been there, you'll know what I mean. If not, you'll either know soon enough, or remain entrenched drowning in your own resentment poo. Don't do the latter, you can do so much better.

RULES FOR SURVIVAL: THERE ARE NO PROBLEMS, ONLY SOLUTIONS.

Rule #1: 'Blame' yourself (aka *empower* yourself)! Blaming others may be instantly gratifying, it's also utterly useless and very unemancipated. It's like the baby having a tantrum, or the small child nagging. It makes you feel somewhat relieved in the instant. But if the other party doesn't solve your problem you'll remain trapped in a vicious circle of frustration and bitterness. And if they *do* solve the problem, you may think all is well, but in reality you remain dependent on them.

The far better solution is, in every situation that is less than ideal, to think for yourself: "What can *I* do to solve this problem *myself*, or prevent it in the future?" If you take the carton of orange juice from the fridge and start shaking it, and the sticky liquid splashes all over you because the person before you didn't screw on the cap properly, don't go into a tantrum blaming and cursing them, and don't even try to educate them to a higher level of juice carton closing. Simply consider that *you* can easily check if the carton is correctly closed before you start shaking it. This solves the problem from now until eternity, with the added advantage that you're in charge now, instead of at the mercy of their good will and mindfulness (and carton closing skills). **Take them and their behavior as a given, and yourself as the variable. That's empowerment.**

Now there are bigger problems in the world than orange juice splattering over you (although admittedly it might not feel like that when it happens), but the general principle remains the same. Does your job suck? Stop blaming your narcissistic manager, your colleague with the sewer breath or the selfish customers. Start taking *them* as a *given* and see what *you* can do in this wide world full of possibilities. Are people f*ing up the planet? Take them as a given, and see what you can do, with their neurobiological characteristics as a given. Are they shortsighted, selfish, materialistic and indifferent? Take that as a given, and see how you should behave within that context.

Rule #2: Gratefully receive the fabulous gift of *limited choice* (and stop wanting to have your cake *and* eat it). This Universe has certain equilibriums, certain limits you can't just make disappear. Embrace them and redirect your energy elsewhere instead of fretting about them. Limitations are the spice of life.

You can't for instance pass your entire days eating pizza and guzzling cola on the couch, *and* maintain or even less grow a tight six-pack abdomen at the same time. Maybe in some other Universe it's possible, but you don't have access to it. At the very least you'd have to die first. In *this* universe, you have the fabulous gift of *limited choice*: *either* gorge on pizzas and cola, *or* flaunt the six-pack, it's completely up to you. Forget the '*and*' option. Luckily there are extremely few situations where you have no choice at all. There are always things you can let go off, and instantly new options will appear. Your mind delivers the ultimate freedom.

HOMO NEUROTIPICUS: WHO THEY ARE AND HOW TO HANDLE THEM?

Now we've got our foundations in order and have a thorough grasp of the three root causes of our unhappiness, it's time to put on our explorer's gear and grab our binoculars, a pair of tweezers and a notebook, because we're going on a zoologist's expedition into *Homo neurotipicus* territory. It's safari time!

We're going to describe *Homo neurotipicus'* quirks and characteristics, its weird habits, its twisted 'normality' and extraordinary conformity to the standard. The goal? Just like a primatologist needs to know enough about the species they're investigating before being able to safety venture into its cage or natural habitat, and certainly before engaging in interaction with them, *we* need to become aware of how exactly, and if possible *why* exactly, our good friends *Homo neurotipicus* do what they do, don't do what they don't do, think what they think, and say what they say.

We neurodivergents are going to share the same, small

planet with them for a long time to come, so we'd better get to know them and learn how to efficiently handle our interactions with them, instead of continuing to drown in vicious circles of false expectations, deception, frustration, disappointment, depression, and false hope. Armed with the right knowledge and a good dose of relativism, there's not much that can stop us. So here we go, to boldly describe *Homo neurotipicus* like no one has described them before.

A WORD OF WARNING (SUPERIORITY/INFERIORITY THINKERS, YOU'VE COME TO THE WRONG ADDRESS!)

Before we begin the central piece of our journey, let's be very clear on one thing right from the start. I like to make good fun of those irritating neurotypicals. But when I say 'handle neurotypicals' or 'deal with neurotypicals,' I don't mean like 'once and for all' in some kind of mobster jargon or mad scientist's dribble (insert creepy, hollow laughter here and a few lightning bolts emanating from a strange contraption). If you're into mass annihilation, dictatorship, tinkering with people's brains or bodies in ways they didn't ask for, or that in any way compromise their physical or mental integrity, or any other practice or idea that would fit nicely in certain German or Italian ideologies that were especially popular in the first half of the 20th century, you have come to the wrong place and you will find no recipes to satisfy your sadistic urges here. The same goes if you're into personal or group superiority of any kind.

Read my lips. There's no superior or inferior life or life form of any kind; there are only *differences*.

What this book is about is observing, analyzing and recognizing these differences, taking them into account, fully respecting each and every one of them and their right to exist, and find the best possible way, for everyone involved, to co-exist. Not necessarily cuddled together like spoons in a drawer or mackerels in a can, but still co-exist, like in: I exist in this universe, somewhere, and so do they, somewhere. We co-exist.

Hey, but wait. Didn't I say that neurotypicals can be a pain in the rear? Isn't that saying that they're inferior? No, it's not. I don't necessarily always revel in the idea of spending large amounts of time with large quantities of neurotypicals tightly packed together, but that has nothing to do with inferiority or superiority. Aversion or attraction are basic biological realities that as such have nothing to do with inferiority or superiority. Newborn babies display aversion and attraction, and they can hardly be accused of ideas of superiority.

Actually, we neurodivergents notoriously struggle with these issues and often waver between a false sense of superiority ("they're stupid assholes") and a false sense of inferiority ("I'm such a maladjusted weirdo"), ending up confused and insecure. In reality, both superiority and inferiority, in an absolute sense, are useless, senseless and irrelevant concepts. Nothing can be absolutely inferior or superior, *as a whole*, compared with anything else. It all depends on what isolated aspect you're comparing. A rubber band is superior to a stone in elasticity, and inferior in weight. Or is it inferior in rigidity and superior in lightness? And one may be more brownish and the other rather grayish. Depending on your favorite color, one will be superior and the other inferior. So is the rubber band as a whole superior or inferior to the stone? The question doesn't make sense, and neither do thoughts about the superiority or inferiority of one human, type of human, type of brain or intellect, life form, group, or individual compared to another. In essence, all nonsense about superiority and inferiority is just that, nonsense, and that's all there's to it.

So all confusion aside and duly liberated of any lingering hallucinations about superiority and inferiority, let's kick start our exploration and proceed to the different ways in which we, the neurodivergent, can handle neurotypicals, in mutually beneficial ways.

WHY STUDY THEM? (AND WHAT HAPPENS IF WE DON'T?)

When we feel bad, or have the impression we don't fit in the (neurotypical) world or the (neurotypical) world doesn't fit us, there are two main strategies we typically adopt: a) we (try to) change ourselves, or b) we (try to) change them. (Or we sulk, but there's not much to say about that one.) Neither is wise actually, and I'm going to present a third option as the sensible alternative.

BAD STRATEGY NUMBER ONE: SUICIDE WITHOUT A CORPSE

When we adopt the first strategy, namely changing ourselves, we reformat ourselves. We try to become someone who has the necessary characteristics to make life among neurotypicals bearable. Like being blind, deaf, dumb, and senseless, or simply terminally comatose. (Just kidding.)

We try to become a more neurotypical person actually, and although at times it may feel as if we've partly succeeded, in the end we have to admit failure. Otherwise, you wouldn't be reading this book, and I wouldn't have written it. Worse still, every success in this endeavour is actually, on a profound level, a terrible failure on its own. Let me explain.

Changing ourselves is a problematic strategy for various reasons.

To begin with, it's extremely hard. First because many of our personality traits and characteristics are deeply ingrained in our individual biology, much deeper than we think. Many are heavily influenced or at least partially defined by the structure, chemistry, and specific functioning of our individual brain. Yes, there *is* such a thing as brain plasticity: your brain isn't set in stone, it can adapt. But the margin of change our biology allows for is quite limited, and change in this area doesn't come easy or overnight. (It's for this same reason that New Year's resolutions tend to be recurrent and without lasting effect.) Second, our personality traits, habits, and mental tics also correspond with a lot of heavy psychological stuff that lives in the deep and dark waters under the radar of our consciousness. Expectations of parents and peers, childhood traumas big and small, they all have a considerable influence on us of which we're mostly completely unaware. So just 'deciding' or wanting to change is far from enough. It may seem to work for a little while to some degree, but inevitably we revert, as our biology and unconscious psychological content take over the reins again.

Another reason why changing ourselves is problematic, is that we very easily slide down the slippery slope of *over*adaptation. This is especially dramatic for neuro-divergents. If we persist in changing ourselves at all costs, stage two of the self-overhaul project consists of zealously constructing a granite mold of the perfect 'me' and then forcefully squeezing ourselves in it. It gets a bit violent. To pull off this feat, we'll use any kind of high pressure we can find on the abundant spiritual, self-help and self-improvement market. But, just like the greater part of a perfectly nice, well-rounded, adult female behind refuses to enter some ridiculously tight jeans that are made for 15-year-old anorexic girls, there's a considerable quantity of 'me' that will refuse to enter this mold - even with all that mental pressure applied. We then proceed to attack this hated part of ourselves with the steak knife of even more advanced self-improvement techniques, psycho-active substances and therapy, combined with a sturdy pair of mental eye winkers in the form of torrents of feel-good quotes and popular books. I think you're starting to see why I call this *over*adaptation, as opposed to simply adaptation.

Now don't get me wrong. I *do* think there's room for self-improvement in the sense that we all carry a lot of shit from our past that we can, and should, happily sort out. We all have a lot of mental knots and twists that, once unraveled,

make life so much easier and pleasant. But that's *heal.*
overadapting like the pressure mold technique
described above.

The difference between a (self-)healing path and an
overadapting path isn't always easy to tell, not by yourself.
But if you look at it in the following way, you'll easily tell the
two apart.

Healing is a process of becoming who *you are, whoever*
that is, in your most natural form. It's a process of giving
room, of resting, and of getting to know yourself with a
friendly, benevolent curiosity and a really open mind. You
accept whatever you find in yourself and give it all the room
it needs. It's not easy, and it takes time (actually a lifetime)
because there's precisely no objective other than unfolding,
and you'll encounter a lot of stuff that you won't know how
to handle at first. But it should have the taste of adventure,
like a gaining of space, instead of an augmenting pressure.
Sometimes the process is breathtakingly fabulous, sometimes
it's scary and confusing, but at the end of the day the journey,
as a whole, is wonderful. It carries the sensation of a
deepening friendship with yourself, including accepting and
even liking the rough edges, a main characteristic of all true
friendships. It shouldn't seem like a hyper-demanding ultra-
severe education by a sadistic Jesuit that never takes his
piercing eyes of you and is ready to sneak up on you from
behind every corner, ruler in hand to measure and punish
you at will. Nor should you experience it like an endless,
fierce beauty contest or Nobel Prize competition with
yourself and/or the rest of the world. Healing is being
yourself, right now, and becoming gradually more and more
comfortable with that.

Overadapting, on the other hand, is becoming who you
think you *should* be, in your hypothetical most perfect form,
which is the exact opposite of healing. It's forceful and tiring,
and feels like a long, long failure interspersed with the
occasional victory (over your poor natural Self mainly) that
in the end doesn't even last long enough to savor. One can

become addicted to these little victories *and* to the suffering in between. It so happens that the brain prefers a familiar shithole to a potentially happy unknown. And, as every game-addict will know, it's also notoriously keen on the little spikes of dopamine that are released when you reach the next level (be it in a video game, or in your mold-fitting endeavor). This makes it daunting to get out of your self-created sadistic Jesuit boarding school - but not impossible either. Once you have identified your shackles and understood how they work, it's easy to slip out of them. You may need to do this recurrently, especially in the beginning when they slip themselves on again without you even noticing.

The question that takes all of this a little deeper is: where does this image of a more perfect 'me' come from? Before you read on, take a moment to reflect on this.

No, don't read on, think about it yourself.

Okay.

So what did you come up with?

If you dig deep and arduously enough, you'll find that it comes from ... *them*. It's *their* conscious and unconscious unrelenting pressure, *their* rejection of your neurodivergent 'you' and *their* continuous desire for a 'you' that's more convenient for them, that planted this seed in you of feeling not good enough as you are. They don't just plant it, they water it, too, all the time. And now the seed has grown into a jungle vine suffocating your very life. Who is 'them' exactly? That differs from person to person, but usually you shouldn't look far. For neurodivergents, neurotypicals are always a major 'they'.

To make things worse, however perfectly you adapt and then overadapt, there is no scenario where you overadapt *and* get to live a meaningful, happy life. There's no happy ending to overadaptation, for anyone concerned.

If you're overadapting, you'll inevitably lack authenticity. That's exactly the very essence of overadaptation: instead of being your authentic you, you 'are' someone else. This very lack of authenticity is perceived by most people, consciously or unconsciously, as something disagreeable and a sign of untrustworthiness. If you overadapt you'll never really make it into the hearts of other people. They'll intuitively 'smell' a lack of backbone, a failure to dare to be who you really are. A successful complete (over)adaptation, if that's possible to begin with, actually ensures that no-one will ever respect or really love you.

A complete overadaptation where you perfectly correspond to all of their desires is biologically impossible. But let us, for the sake of the argument, assume you pull it off. What would you have accomplished then? A suicide. A murder without a corpse, because the corpse is still walking around, talking (like *they* want it to talk), smiling (like *they* want it to smile) and doing whatever else your persona does or doesn't do, like a programmed puppet. They cannot love or respect *you*, because *you* disappeared behind the overadaptation puppet. It's the puppet, the walking, talking corpse they appreciate, while somewhere in the depths of your mind and body the real you is rotting away, unloved and repressed in the dungeon you relegated it to, hated even by the remainder of yourself.

In short: whether you succeed or not in overadapting yourself to them, either way, you lose.

So, overadaptation? Thanks, but... no thanks. They'll have to cope with me exactly as I am. And if they can't? Well, the world is a big place and I'm not forcing anyone to remain close to me. It's up to them to either choose to remain around me and deal with who I am, or go look for someone else who *does* coincide with their desires and expectations.

BAD STRATEGY NUMBER TWO: THE PETTY DICTATOR

The second strategy is to reformat *them* and turn *them* into a whole new sort of person. Someone completely different from the typical neurotypical they now are. Someone to whom adjectives like smart, compassionate, understanding, open, cooperative, and honest apply, to name just a few. You know, the little things that would make life with them just a tad nicer.

The tactics in this department are probably as old as humankinds are themselves. (Yes, the 's' at the end of 'humankinds' is there for a reason)

There's song and dance, aka 'sensitizing'. This can be literal or metaphorical singing and dancing, bringing heartrending messages about love, empathy, altruism, environmentalism and so on, typically brought in appallingly self-enriching, materialistic and non-environmentally friendly ways by people with appallingly narcissistic, materialistic and non-environmentally friendly ways of life. The whole show typically has next to zero actual effect - apart from nourishing a few bank accounts and narcissistic ego's, and a considerable environmental devastation of course. The sensitizing tactic can also take the form of books, movies, plays, and people shouting on top of soap boxes, to name a few. The bottom line is: all this show and dance has a definite effect, especially on bank accounts and egos, but as a way of causing a profound and lasting change in the personality traits and characteristics of large masses of people, they're an utter failure.

A second tactic is force-feeding people ideologies that are completely alien to their natural inclinations. This is commonly referred to as 'a good education.' A subcategory of this tactic is 'informing', or in other words: hitting people over the head with information they can't really process, and then stand by hoping they'll finally do something smart with it. It doesn't work either. Need convincing? Look around. Given the amount of well-educated and highly informed people scouring the Earth wreaking havoc, I rest my case and let the evidence speak for itself.

And finally, in this non-exhaustive list, there's bribing

them. Like letting subventions, tax deductions, and incentives loose on them. Oh yes, it works. As long as the bribing continues, that is. Sadly, there aren't enough resources to bribe most of the people most of the time. And although bribing may statistically give the impression that people suddenly developed an environmental or social conscience, in the end, once the bribing finished, this marvelous change also disappears and everything reverts to the terrible way it was before. So, in the end, another failure.

Usually, after having tried several of these tactics over an extended period of time, we notice that the information we gave them went in one ear and straight out the other (because the hardware in between their ears isn't capable of capturing it); that once the bribing and the song and dance stop, so does their reaction to them (well, what did we expect really?); and that somehow the force-feeding actually never reached their deep brain structures ('deep' being a relative concept here) and only taught them to fake it better. Sigh.

But we don't give up that easily, oh no! We shift gears and launch phase two.

Phase two of the process consists of simply doing much more of what didn't work, hoping that an overdose will do the job. More singing, more dancing, more educating, informing and bribing, and then, filled with anxious hope, waiting for the effect to happen this time. Of course, more of a bad strategy never won a war.

Don't be misled in thinking that only dumb people indulge in doing more of what *didn't* work, entertaining high hopes that this will solve the problem. Actually, most people fall into this pitfall independently of how smart they are, because being smart is not the same as being wise. Wisdom comes with being smart *and* having been sufficiently hit in the face by Reality (the latter seems to be equipped with a huge baseball bat attached to a tireless robot arm for this purpose), and even then, only a minority actually gives up the 'rinse and repeat' process, sits down, and rethinks it all.

Those who don't wise up (being the majority of world improvers) turn gradually into dogmatic and obsessive mini-dictators who, each time more bitterly and aggressively, try to force people into becoming something they simply can't become. You can manipulate, educate, inform, bribe, punish, reward, and sensitize a chimp all you want, it'll never become a bonobo for it. Either it'll remain as good as unaffected, or it'll tear your head off, or it'll become a freak - but it'll always remain a chimp.

These mini-dictators also become notoriously allergic to reality checks. They are addicted to what they call 'hope', but which actually is nothing more than their own pathetic clinging to a psychotic dream of a world that fits their personal needs. Like with any other type of hard addiction or psychosis, it becomes gradually more difficult to get through to these people as they entrench themselves deeper and deeper in their sickness. Most of them never get out and simply die mentally addicted and subclinically psychotic, all the while loudly blaming everyone and everything but themselves for the cosmic injustice they've had to endure.

If you recognize yourself somewhat in this profile, don't despair, you're not too far lost yet, because at least you still *recognize* yourself. So quickly move on to the sensible alternative, described below, and all will be well soon, with you, with the world, and between the two of you.

THE SENSIBLE ALTERNATIVE

So both in adapting *them* to our needs and (over)adapting *ourselves* to their needs, we try, we fail, and most times we try more of the same. With enough repetition we fade away and literally or figuratively become worm food.

Or ... we get out of the merry-go-round and do something else entirely.

But what's the alternative? A mix of radical personal honesty, waking up to reality and adopting a scientific, zoological approach to our neurotypical scourge. The three together are also commonly known as: *getting real*.

To start with, take 'them' as a given. (See also the advice at the end of *Root cause #1: The Perception Paradox* above). Yes, it's a mournful experience, letting the idea sink into you that 'they' will never change. It's mournful *at first*, at least. But once you boldly choose this door and pass the obligatory mourning stages, you'll find that a whole new source of almost boundless energy awaits you. Why? Because instead of wasting your precious life force into trying to change them, with next to no effect apart from your own exhaustion and growing bitterness, you'll discover all this energy at your complete disposal for whatever else you may want to do. Like living a full, real, f*ing great life for a change. You'll see that right from the beginning, you'll suddenly find yourself with such an excess of energy, time and space instead of the usual exhaustion, that you won't even know where to start.

If this doesn't convince you, here are three very good reasons for stopping all attempts to change them. (The first two were already treated earlier on, but for the sake of completeness I'll very briefly go over them again.)

To begin with, you're not the only one, and maybe not even the smartest one, to have tried changing them. Countless generations have come before you trying the exact same thing, including people just as smart and smarter than you, and countless others are trying to do the same at this very moment. They didn't succeed, they aren't succeeding. Chances are it's a strategy that's doomed from the start. So I say: drop that. New beginnings. Reevaluate, start over, take a different approach altogether, from the ground up.

Second of all, you're not the only one trying to influence them. The chance of them moving in *your* direction is very slim indeed. Especially because your direction is counternatural for them, which makes those chances even slimmer.

Third, and most importantly actually, you don't *need* them to change. You *think* you do, because you're obsessed with a dream of a planet where they're different and you're happy because they're different. Drop the obsession, take a deep breath, open your eyes to reality *as it is*, and feel how you can cope with it *if only you take it as it is*. You're not stupid, you have plenty of superb characteristics which make you more than apt to deal with whatever the universe throws your way, be it neurotypical or other. Yes, you have your limitations, but once you really get to know and accept them, they'll be easy to cope with and might even prove useful or outright become your very special force. (The famous kung fu fighter Bruce Lee developed his especially badass flying kick on the basis of one leg being significantly shorter than the other.) If you don't succeed in handling things, it's not because you can't, it's because you don't see them as they are. Partly because of the three root characteristics as described earlier, partly because you're simply too busy dreaming of your perfect world in order to see them.

So get real, take them as a given, stop your childish obsession with changing them to your liking, and get out there as the powerful man or woman you actually are.

Then, once you take them as a given, study them as they are. Don't study them with the objective to change them. Study them in order to *know* them - *as they are*. If you're observing them clearly and simply, not hampered by your own dreams of how they *should* be, they're not complicated at all. Compared to you, a neurodivergent, these neurotypicals are definitely different. But different doesn't mean you can't find sense and yes, even logic in them (who would have thought that, right?). And once you get that, you're empowered beyond what you think possible now.

And aren't you the lucky bastard! Studying them and understanding them happens to be exactly what we're going to do in the next chapters.

CHARACTERISTICS OF *HOMO NEUROTIPICUS*

"SO WHAT THE HELL IS WRONG WITH THESE F*ING NEUROTYPICALS ANYWAY?!?"

Have you ever thought "So what the hell is wrong with these f*ing neurotypicals anyway?!?"?

I have.

I know it doesn't feel like that, but there's actually nothing *wrong* with neurotypicals, just like there's nothing *wrong* with the mosquitos in your bedroom, the moles in your garden, chimps, dolphins, or three weeks of rain during your summer holiday.

Nothing at all? Not even a tiny bit of something? No. Nothing.

The next sentence may sound uncomfortable at first, but it's actually the key to emancipation, so bear with me. What is wrong, if you're unhappy with neurotypicals, is *your* way of seeing them and seeing yourself, and *your* expectations of them and yourself. Your mental landscape doesn't coincide with the real world in front of you, and that can only lead to disaster.

Does this feel like the blame for everything going wrong in your world falls on you now, instead of on those f*ng normies? Well, it should and it shouldn't. It should because the focal point is indeed you here. But it shouldn't because 'blame' is not the right word. I'm not going to overload you with guilt. Instead, I'm into **giving you all the tools you need to become an empowered, autonomous man or woman.** Let's get those muscles rolling and open that big oyster of a world! But first, a paradigm shift.

Homo neurotipicus is not innately 'bad'. They do however have some characteristics that make life with them a challenge. Okay, let's be honest, and call it a nightmare. It's like we're in an arranged wedding with them, packed together in close quarters and expected to get along perfectly, while in reality it's not that easy. At all.

To make things even worse, from *their* point of view it's not any better. In *their* eyes we neurodivergents are a minority of obnoxious weirdo's who make their lives f*ing complicated. In their minds we suffer from an annoying, deep and unresolvable *otherness* which they thoroughly dislike. As *they* see it, we indulge in obsessive nagging (when we insist on saving them from their own stupidities); snottily pointing out every one of their inconsistencies and mistakes (when we disregard their ego games and simply state facts as they are); always asking uncomfortable questions upsetting their nicely established pecking orders (like when you ask a teacher or a professor a question that's smarter than they can handle); and in general being smart-ass know-it-all pesky nerds who seem to be intent on shaming every mistake they ever make and thwarting their every effort to look better than they really are. If you were a neurotypical, you wouldn't enjoy seeing a neurodivergent coming your way either. (Except of course when we neurodivergents overadapt and crawl at their feet in groveling servitude, as explained earlier.)

If you take us, neurodivergents, out of the picture for a moment, neurotypicals are perfectly okay. Yes, they really are! You may think they're too dumb to even survive as a species, but they're actually, *in their own way*, well-balanced and exactly smart enough to handle their own world really well. They solve overpopulation with dismal hygiene, diseases, and wars. They solve social conflicts with faking, lying and what primatologists call grooming. They solve uncertainty with superstition and actually believe in magic and miracles, and in *their* logic, it all makes perfect sense. And they invent only what they can handle (by definition), which are quite simple technologies that can't do much harm to ecosystems, or even to large groups of people at the same time. (Think sticks and stones, wooden spears and clubs, and punches in the face, instead of atom bombs, pesticides, fracking, and endocrine-disrupting chemicals).

If you put neurodivergent hi-tech in neurotypical hands however, stuff they could never invent themselves and actually don't understand but are happy to (mis)use for their own neurotypical objectives, things get out of hand quickly. This makes it seem that they're not even capable of properly surviving as a life form. But are they? Or is it *us*, neurodivergents, who are guilty of putting technology in their hands they cannot possibly handle in a responsible manner, because they cannot possibly anticipate all the consequences of using this 'alien' tech?

As a life form there's nothing wrong with them as such. And it's not as if there is something wrong with us neurodivergents either. It's just that them and us, we're not very *compatible*. Not in every configuration, that is.

Life forms of extremely different characteristics co-exist on this planet and are actually closely knit in a giant texture of interdependence. We can perfectly well share the planet with those, so we can perfectly well share the planet with our neurotypical friends too. But maybe not tied together by an arm and a leg, like we are today. And certainly not projecting characteristics upon them that they don't have.

Maybe we need a little more space, mutually, and certainly we, *neurodivergents*, need a much clearer vision of *them*. If they can't understand us, that's fine. But given that it's us, neurodivergents, who are capable of bringing a lot of weird tech and 'complications' into this world, perhaps *we* at least have to understand *them*, be the wiser party and act accordingly.

So let's get to know this *Homo neurotipicus*, and see how we can organize things for the better. Join me as we ruffle through the notes of my ethological field trips in *Homo neurotipicus* territory, and make sense of what seems to have none.

THEY LIVE IN TINY MENTAL BUBBLES

MENTAL WHAT?

Every being with a mind lives in a kind of mental bubble.

What do I mean by 'mental bubble'? Well, it's obviously impossible for any sentient being to take *all* phenomena, across *all* of time and space, continuously into consideration. We all have a kind of mental horizon. Anything beyond our mental horizon, beyond the outer surface of what I call 'our mental bubble,' escapes our attention and our consideration, as if it didn't exist.

Let's represent a person's mental bubble symbolically as a circle, like in the image below. Meet Joe, inside his mental bubble.

Now let's represent some of the things inside and outside Joe's mental bubble.

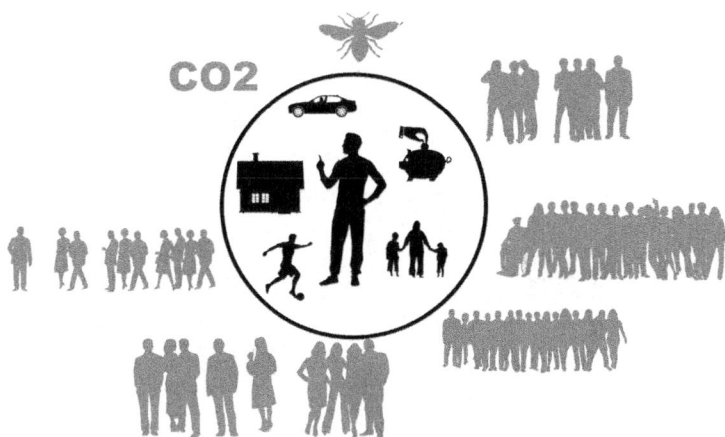

We can see that Joe is well aware of his car, his house, the soccer competition, his bank account, and his wife and children (to *some* extent, that is). Those are all inside the circle representing the horizon of his mind, and they play a significant part in all of his decisions and thoughts. He is *not* aware however of the greenhouse effect of carbon dioxide, nor of the problem of bees massively dying off (and certainly not of the effect his car and his house have on the bees, nor of the bees on the food he buys). Most other people on this planet fall outside of his mental bubble, too.

ONE SIZE DOESN'T FIT ALL

The crucial thing to understand about humans is that the size of their mental bubble varies greatly from one individual to another.

Let's take a look at Jane, for instance, inside her more spacious mental bubble.

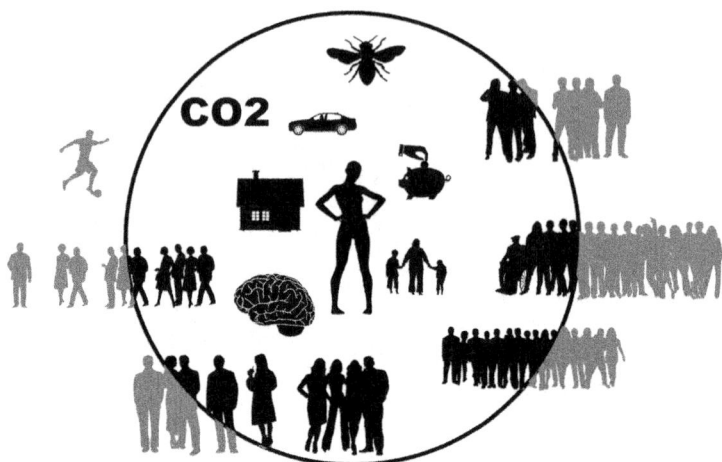

Jane is, just like Joe, aware of her car, her house, her family and her bank account. But contrary to Joe she also takes into account, in all her decisions and thoughts, a lot of other people nearby and far-off; and carbon dioxide emissions (she probably has a more environmental friendly car than Joe, or is thinking of swapping it for a bike and a train season ticket altogether); and the bees dying (Jane buys organic food to support farmers who don't use bee-killing pesticides). Jane is not really aware of what's going on in the world of soccer, but instead she's into neuroscience. I'll admit I kind of like Jane. She's cool.

Most people would call Joe somewhat more egotistical than Jane. I would call him *mentally nearsighted*, compared to Jane. Or I would say: "his mental bubble is smaller."

If you could stick a number on the size of people's mental bubbles, and plot those in a graph, it would very probably (like many other human characteristics) look like a bell curve.

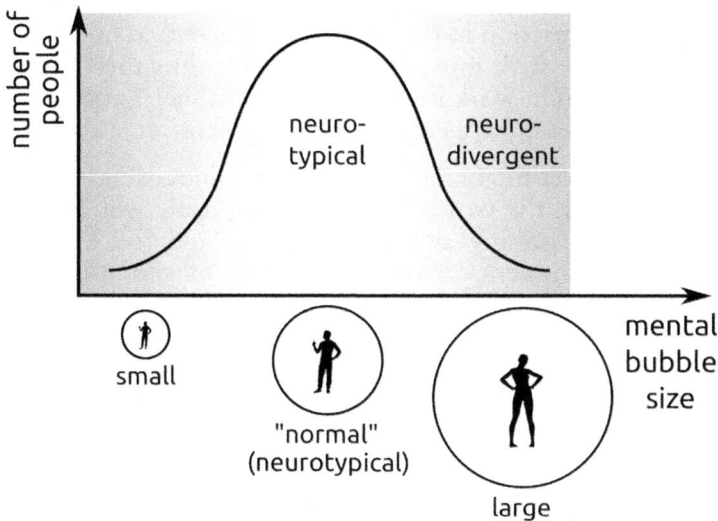

Most people, by definition, have an average sized mental bubble. That's the chunky part in the middle of the curve, eternal home to neurotypicals. To the left of the graph we have a minority of people who have a tiny mental bubble. These would include low-functioning autistic people for instance, and people with an intellectual disability. To the right of the graph, there are the neurodivergents with an especially large mental bubble. These include the high IQ people, the especially creative, the highly empathetic, et cetera. The ones that "complicate everything," "think too much," make "impossible" connections between (to neurotypicals) seemingly unrelated things, et cetera. Definitely neurodivergent. Definitely a minority. Definitely not understood by your average neurotypical.

In our examples above, Joe would sit somewhere in the middle of the curve, and Jane would find herself somewhere to the right.

Joe would feel quite in place on this planet, since most people have a mental bubble roughly the same size as his.

They enjoy the same kind of jokes he does, they have the same general reaction to the same kind of events as him. They might disagree with him on certain topics, but their mental machinery would work in similar ways and their mutual way of thinking would happen in the same dimension.

Jane however might feel at times as if some cosmic mistake planted her on the wrong planet. Most people would deem her way of reasoning awkward. They would feel as if she hauls in arguments from nowhere, maybe find her hypersensitive, and generally consider that she complicates everything too much. If Jane doesn't overadapt, others will probably not find her fun to hang out with. If she does overadapt, she can be fun to others but there'll be no fun in it for her. And as long as she unconsciously thinks that everyone has the same size of mental bubble as she has, she'll be in for a generous daily serving of frustration, anger, confusion, misunderstanding, and depression.

Let's take the example of the bees dying. This issue is well within Jane's mental horizon, but falls outside of Joe's scope. When Jane talks about this to Joe, he tunes out, answers with platitudes, and brings up manifestly faulty arguments. He might even get upset. It's not that Joe doesn't know what a bee is, what pesticides are, or that he can't have a muzzy understanding of 'pesticides kill bees'. But his mental bubble is too small to accommodate his car, the soccer league *and* the whole, actually rather complex issue of bees, agriculture, food supply, health, etcetera. And if something has to be thrown out of Joe's mental bubble, it's not going to be the car or the soccer league. They bring all the fun in his life (and that of his equally mentally nearsighted drinking buddies). It's going to be the bees that get axed (mentally, and as a consequence, also physically).

But even if Joe *would* throw out the car and the soccer from his mental bubble, the whole bee issue wouldn't fit in anyway. Because if you look at it objectively, environmental issues are of the most complex there are. They include biological, chemical, engineering, sociological and psychological aspects, extrapolations, and multiple mathematical models, all intermingled in quite complicated ways; and if the bees dying out seems a rather straightforward issue to you with your neurodivergent brain, it might be way over Joe's head. Although (and this is a very important part to understand) he'll never admit this because that would lower his social status and prestige.

So if Jane wants to avoid a daily dose of frustration and depression, she will have to consciously realize that Joe's head simply isn't made for dying bee issues, and divert her energy elsewhere, other than toward Joe's poor little brain that's already overworked as it is with the car, the soccer and the bank account. (Luckily Jane is into neuroscience, so she should be able to get this quickly, once pointed in the right direction.)

Rule for survival: One mental size doesn't fit all. Be *acutely* aware that most people's mental bubble differs substantially from yours. Just don't expect them to admit it, or even realize it. Don't waste your time and energy on people who don't actively think *with* you on any subject. If they're basically just nodding, just nay-saying, just repeating, just getting upset, or just spewing out falsehoods and platitudes, stop right there and walk away, or talk about the weather (briefly). They're not getting it and won't ever get it because it doesn't fit in their head. Their biological brain isn't made for accommodating everything your brain can accommodate.

JUGGLING THEIR BALLS

The differences in mental bubble sizes can be illustrated by another image, namely that of (mental) juggling: how many items does one have in mind at the same time when considering an issue, and how diverse are these items? By items, I mean ideas, observations, and concepts. At a very basic physiological level, they're actually neural firings in different brain areas: speech-related, mathematical, abstract, sensory, motricity-related, emotional, et cetera. Two parameters are essential here: 1) *how much* simultaneous firing is there at any point (is it a Christmas tree or rather one lonely, slowly blinking led at a time)? and 2) *how diverse* are the brain areas that are lighting up (are we talking purely mathematical for instance, or rather a combination of mathematics, visual imagery, emotions, et cetera)?

In the mental juggling metaphor, a person with a low score on both parameters would be 'juggling' one ball, over and over again - if you still can call that 'juggling' of course. They're a minority that includes, apart from most individuals of simply low intelligence, also the linear, serial thinkers. The latter can seem very intelligent in certain aspects of logic and reasoning but are very limited in what they can understand and accomplish on the whole.

Most people would have medium scores on both parameters, juggling a few mental items that are somewhat diverse. (I'm looking at you, neurotypical).

And then there's another minority of neurodivergents that can juggle an exceptional quantity of mental items that are (to neurotypicals at least) mindbogglingly diverse. These are the creative, out-of-the-box, innovative thinkers with a really broad interest. Their thinking is fabulously interesting and a joy to follow for people like them, but to those in the other categories it tends to be overly wild, confusing, and outright incomprehensible.

Again, this isn't a case of one kind of mental juggling

being better or worse than the other. Instead, it's about *differences*, about knowing them, acknowledging them, and learning how to handle them best.

In the image below, I illustrated two kinds of mental juggling. The (neurotypical) man to the left is juggling his, ahem, two balls (and not even understanding those by the way). The (neurodivergent) man to the right is juggling *his* two balls *and* a ton of stuff related to the environment, scientific data, emotions, other people, thoughts of future effects, etcetera. I'm sure you get exactly what I mean as you've probably met a ton of people like the one depicted on the left, and (hopefully) one or two like the one on the right.

Here, the specter of self-projection (unconsciously assuming that others have the same characteristics as oneself) rears its ugly head again. If you think everyone else mentally juggles as many items from as many diverse dimensions as you do, then you're in for a lot of frustration and misunderstanding.

But this isn't as easy to realize as it seems. Self-projection is a tenacious habit. To those who have a natural ability to mentally juggle lots of items in relatively complex models, doing so doesn't *feel* like "mentally juggling lots of items in relatively complex models." It doesn't *feel* difficult or complex. It feels like simply doing some basic thinking. So if we don't pay close attention, we're at risk of automatically assuming that *everyone* is capable of "mentally juggling lots of items in relatively complex models" because everyone is supposed to be capable of basic thinking.

Remember the example of Joe and the dying bees? What do you think will happen if we obstinately keep assuming that he can, or even wants to, mentally juggle more than he can actually handle? Are we doing the bees a favor? Are we doing ourselves, or even Joe, a favor?

One size of mental bubble definitely doesn't fit all; and as a neurodivergent either you acknowledge that fact, or you remain Captain Disaster.

Rule for survival: Mental mileage may vary. Not everyone can juggle as many mental items as you, or the same diversity of items. Avoid disasters: don't throw too much at them. (And remember that 'not very much' for us, is often way too much for them). If you throw more at them than they can handle, they'll feel overwhelmed, looked down upon, tested beyond their limits, or even attacked. Wouldn't you, if someone keeps throwing stuff at you, in rapid succession, that you can't handle? The problem is that they'll almost never admit to their incapacity. Avoid disaster for yourself and the world, and be wise enough to take their limits into account. They won't, but you can.

WOBBLY, NOT STRETCHY

People's mental bubbles are dynamic in form: as the conscious and unconscious mental focus travels from one subject to the other, the mental bubble accordingly bulges out in some places and retracts in others, much like a big soap bubble that travels through the windy air outside.

In the illustrations below, the gray outline signifies the

original form and size of the mental bubble, and the black outline represents how it can change.

This happens.
(Form changes, size remains the same)

But in our understanding of people, and especially of neurotypicals, it's really important to observe that the overall *size* (or volume if you like) of most adults' mental bubble hardly changes over time. Their bubble wobbles about; in reality, it may expand a bit in some directions to the expense of a retraction in other places, but its *overall* size, for *most* people, remains roughly the same.

This happens.
(Small change in size)

This doesn't happen (in neurotypicals).
(Significant increase in size)

Just like many other characteristics that are rooted in neurobiology, there's great variation in the individual capacity of growth of this mental bubble. It would probably result in another bell curve when graphed for the entire human population.

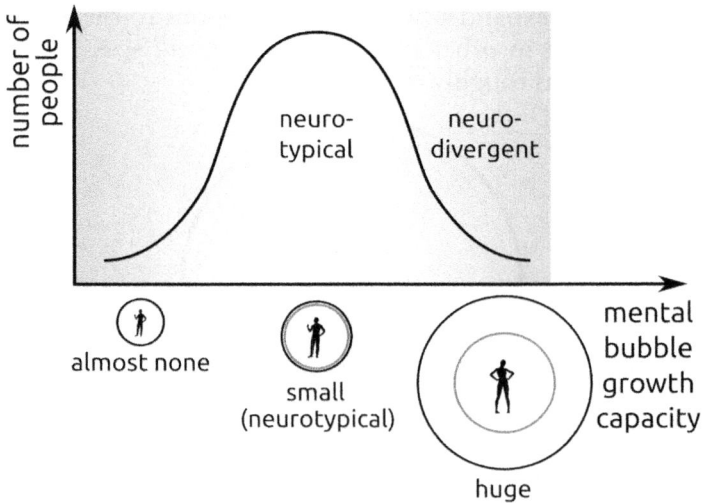

To the left of the graph there's a minority whose maximum mental bubble size is small, and completely and thoroughly fixed.

And who do we find in the merry middle? Yes, you guessed that right: our good friends, the neurotypicals again. There they are, back-slapping each other, having good ole jolly fun trampling about and living life just like prehistoric times were yesterday, only with windows in their caves this time, and horses with gear sticks and steering wheels! Their mental bubble is slightly stretchy, although the effort to expand it can be painful to them at times. It can't grow much, mind you, otherwise history wouldn't repeat itself. But it can expand just enough to learn how to operate a smartphone, or transition from cassettes to CD's to MP3's for instance.

You spotted your own, neurodivergent home in the graph already, of course. To the right, there are those of us whose mental bubble can actually increase in size almost indefinitely, as long as we live. Here you find the mentally flexible and endlessly evolving individuals who are always eager to learn, who continuously challenge their paradigms and beliefs, and who continue to fine-tune their understanding and awareness as long as they live. We also know that the latter are a deploringly small minority.

Accepting the fact that the mental bubble for most people doesn't significantly grow in size once they have petrified into adulthood, may seem obvious and easy at first sight. But when it concerns our own children, our romantic or business partners, our spouses, parents, friends, neighbors, compatriots, co-voters concerning important political issues, co-workers we'll have to deal with for years to come, et cetera, it may become very difficult to digest that the size of their mental bubble is what it is, and will remain like that, give or take a tiny few percent. At times the bubble they live in may seem so ridiculously, irritatingly, and dangerously small that we *want* to believe that it can be made substantially bigger, so that catastrophes can be averted and things changed for the better. History and close personal observation tell us however - for those who are willing and able to accept the facts - that reality is different, and that most people's mental horizons are almost impossible to significantly widen. There's no real cure for inborn mental nearsightedness yet - because if there were, the world would be a completely different place.

If we *really* want to avert disaster, it won't be by looking *away* from this reality. Only by looking directly *at it* and taking it into account in all of our thoughts and actions can we adequately deal with the situation. Once we accept reality as it is, things invariably become quite easy.

Rule for survival: They're Weebles, not Gumbies! Don't expect people, and especially not neurotypicals, to substantially wise up, expand mentally, or even simply change. Worse even, if they change, it's usually in the degeneration direction, not the wisdom direction. Applying this knowledge in our personal relationships, but also in politics and environmentalism, to name a few, can be a total game changer.

MATTER OVER MIND

This is quite an obvious one, but it's also a fundamental truth. So we need to go over it briefly anyway. Neurotypicals are definitely very materialistic. Not only are the *size* and growth capacity of their mental bubble specific (as in: specifically small), the *kind* of things you'll find inside there are specific, too.

Neurotypicals are often busy pimping their homes, cars, children, and themselves. They love things and luxuries at the expense of all other concerns, even their own health. Have you noticed how obsessively they stuff their homes and bellies, and smear, spray and inject their skins and surfaces, even with harmful materials? How they gladly plague the planet in this quest for maximization of their own consumption? Have you ever wondered how it's possible that they're at the same time embellishing their nest, and shitting all over it? Well, that's the combination of materialism and a tiny mental bubble for you. Look at what they do, instead of listening to them twisting and turning to find a morally acceptable explanation of this gluttonous frenzy, and you'll easily observe that personal, material pleasure is at the top of their one-item list. "More, more, more, for me, me, me" is the Holy Mantra of neurotypicalhood.

In pair with this materialistic mania, neurotypicals don't give a hoot about philosophical questions. They may pretend, if that'll propel them up the social ladder. In that case they'll give embarrassing displays of pseudo-philosophical diarrhea of the mouth that comes right off the backside of grandmother's calendar and makes the more natural philosophers writhe in agony.

As mentioned earlier (remember Joe in his tiny bubble), they can't really be bothered with large-scale issues like peace, the environment, social inequality, et cetera, either. If they could be, wouldn't these issues have long been resolved, or rather never have sprung into existence in the first place?

Rule for survival: remember, matter over mind (for neurotypicals at least). "Mo Money" is the mantra. Don't expect anything from them except "more, more, more stuff, for me, me, me" and don't be deceived into thinking they can be bothered with much else.

Abracadabra

Each New Year neurotypicals ostentatiously wish themselves and the members of their various tribes good health and all the happiness in the world. That over and done with, they immediately start creating all the causes for exactly the opposite to happen. The inexperienced neurotypical-watcher looks at this seemingly odd behavior flabbergasted. But it so happens that health and happiness, just like the intimately related dimension of environmental protection, are complex issues for which one needs a sizable mental bubble and a robust capacity to mentally juggle many concepts at the same time. As explained before, two things neurotypicals are not especially endowed with.

The end result of this mental nearsightedness and cognitive clumsiness is that they're heavily into *magical thinking*, of which their behavior on New Year's Eve is just one small example. Don't be fooled into thinking that a scientific education can cure them of magical thinking. It can't.

When I say "magical thinking," I'm not just referring to obvious, traditional superstitions like lucky T-shirts, lucky numbers, clover, rabbit's foot, Friday the 13th, touching wood, don't talk ill of the dead, don't say a disaster won't happen lest it would befall you, and all that jazz. I'm above all referring to the day-to-day, 'normal' way of using words as if they were magical incantations instead of descriptions.

Let me give some examples. Neurotypicals love to say "It'll pass" or "It'll get better", although nothing at all points in that direction, or even worse, everything points to the contrary. Or "I'll find them, I promise," "I'll come back from the war, I promise," and other kinds of vows that are simply completely unfounded. One can promise to try. But a promise to succeed in these things holds no value whatsoever. If you asked a neurotypical, "which exact observation of cause-and-effect *exactly* makes you say or think that?," they'll be at a complete loss. (*And* they'd think you were an obnoxious nerd.)

Actually, when you do so, you'll get nonsensical answers like "Well, I don't know, I just think so," "everyone knows so," "you never know" (which in their case is quite correct most of the time). Or they'll attack you, spitting things like "what a dumb question is that," or they'll deviate into another subject. They generally actually feel superior for not really bothering with sound observations and cause and effect, and for spewing the same platitudes their cronies spit out. It nurtures a cozy group feeling among them.

In short, many of their utterings aren't observations or realistic descriptions, but rather *incantations*, like magical spells, with which they try to control the "invisible" world of cause and effect outside their mental bubble that at times comes crashing into their lives without them having a clue to how or why. Compare it with a heavily nearsighted person. Imagine something comes flying into their circle of vision, let's say a ball from a group of kids playing outside their field of vision. To the nearsighted person, this ball seems to appear out of nowhere and since he or she couldn't see the beginning of the trajectory, he or she can't anticipate where it's going to fly next to. To their naked, actual perception there seems to be no cause and effect because the cause is completely outside their field of perception. The thing appeared out of nowhere and displays random behavior. While someone with good vision would have seen the ball coming, and can extrapolate its course easily. In the same way it's logical that a neurotypical treats anything that originates outside their mental bubble as "magical," instead of governed by causes and effects. (Again, they'll never admit to this openly, though.)

So, happily smoking along, deeply inhaling tar and other known toxic substances into their lungs, they *wish* themselves and their passively co-smoking children and partner a good health. They may even touch wood to reinforce this magical wish. A year later, they are devastated that the combined effects of smoking, magical utterings and touching wood, turn out to be lung cancer instead of good health. Upon which they burn a candle, or turn to the "magic of science."

Which brings us to a special case of magical thinking: *magical scientific thinking.* This may seem a paradox, but in the neurotypical world it's not. For many neurotypicals, science is the contemporary magic. "Science will solve it" is the typical credo of the magical-scientific believer. It's their omnipotent answer to any and every problem. How will science solve it? They don't know. Are there any indications that science can fix it to begin with, or is even remotely close? They don't know. "Scire", the Latin root of the word "science", means: to know. For being "science" adepts, there's astonishingly little knowledge in their minds. Science is their mystical tower of strength, and the scientist is their priestly connection to the deity of Science. He or she is Its representative on Earth, muttering hermetical formulas that will do the magic they need. Popular articles, which make them believe they understand things they actually don't, are their bible.

Just like other religious groups, neurotypical science-believers will smack you over the head with their deity whenever they can. They superficially reject superstition and other religions (although secretly they may well avoid black cats, and just before dying indulge in some religious ritual because "you never know" some god is out there anyway just waiting to take revenge). Science-believers endow "Science" with the same characteristics others endow *their* superstitions and religions with: omnipotence, and holding the absolute and unshakable truth. (You can't be further away from science than that, actually).

Whether people are into magical thought and speech isn't the key problem. It's *their* lives, they can do with them whatever they want. Whatever rocks their boat. But if you take their magical thought and speech for something it's not, if you think their self-assured statements are being based on observation and sound reflection instead of on superstitious hope and an unconscious belief in magic, if you mistake their "scientific beliefs" for real science or even an interest in real science, you can waste a lot of time and energy, or even a life, much better spent otherwise.

Rule for survival: For neurotypicals, everything is magic – including science. They think predominantly in a 'magical' manner. Don't be fooled into thinking it's any different, and don't take them any more seriously than they deserve. There's also no use in arguing with people who mindlessly mumble incantations (be they scientific or other). Save your breath, saliva and brain power for something more useful. Check the facts for yourself, look into causes and effects, and don't let yourself be carried away by their unfounded enthusiasm or anxiety. And don't think that because they "love science," they actually have any idea of what science is really about.

SELFISHLY SOCIAL

Neurotypicals actually don't care if the Earth turns around the Sun, the Sun around the Earth, or the whole Universe around a giant baboon's ass. In reality, the center of their universe is their own person, so their sphere of interest doesn't reach much farther than that.

But the fulfillment of their burning desires, which are in essence materialistic and very egocentric, is highly dependent on other people. And this makes these other people extremely important to them. Not *as people*, mind you. Not as living, feeling persons whose emotional life and well-being would be of a special interest to them. No, they're interested in others simply because other people tend to influence their own attempts to grab the banana - either facilitating or hindering them.

So while it's true that neurotypicals are obsessed with other humans, don't be fooled into thinking that this makes them exquisitely prosocial, deeply interested in others, or especially empathetic. They're in it for the banana, and for the banana only.

It's quite logical actually. Whenever a neurotypical wants something, there's always one or more other neurotypicals lurking around. Other neurotypicals have very similar material desires to themselves, and this makes them either competitors or allies they have to take into account. Like flies swarming to the yummy piece of fresh shit, neurotypicals gravitate to the same stuff. Their gathering at that point in space and time is not motivated by a drive for real togetherness though. It's the shit in the center that does the gravitational work, to which they respond like magnets. And there they find themselves, "together," and now forced to engage in the complex social hassle to make the best of it and avoid ripping each other's heads off. Those they can bully will be bullied out of the way, those stronger than themselves will be ass-licked or deceived. Alliances will be made and broken, trust will be created and betrayed. You know, the usual. It's all very social, but not all that *sociable* if you look just beneath the surface.

All of this makes neurotypicals very anthropocentric. It all revolves around humans, in a very obsessive and nearsighted way. The easiest way to observe this is in issues concerning environmental protection. It's already extremely difficult to kick a neurotypical into having (or at least feigning) some interest in not-completely-fucking-up-the-planet in general. Due to their mental myopia, it demands a lot of squinting for them to actually notice the environment as a complex *whole* instead of a vague concept. But to kick them into having an interest for environmentalist issues that aren't directly related to human beings, like securing a habitat for animals or trees (especially non-cute, in other words, non-human-like forms of life), you really would have to be a kind of psychological Bruce Lee. Moreover, *if* you succeed, it takes you about an hour of expertly applying your mental martial arts, and the effect lasts for about one minute at most. Not cost-efficient at all. And certainly not pleasant as a pastime.

All this egotism and anthropocentrism, and the corresponding criminal indifference toward other life forms, may seem evil and mean at first sight, but actually it's not. In reality; it's *worse* than that. It's a complete lack of the neurobiological capacity to be caring and smart. If they were evil, maybe there would be some remedy, some therapy, something one could do. It turns out they're stupid and mentally nearsighted, and there's no remedy for that.

It's time for us, neurodivergents, to accept this reality as it is. Nobody blames chimps for not actively protecting endangered species. They're monkeys, we don't expect anything from them except monkey business. We simply accept their mental limits, or more precisely, we actually don't even see them as limits because we never compared them with ourselves to begin with. But on neurotypicals we have this obsession of projecting our own characteristics. Through this projection, or hallucination if you like, we interpret their selfish behavior as meanness and indifference towards other life forms, as if they *can* care, but *won't*. Actually, they simply *can't*, just like they can't fly, or breathe underwater. But deceptive as they are, and given the crucial importance of hierarchical status in their world, they'll never admit to *not being able* to do something.

So there's this feedback circle of 1) us presupposing, or stubbornly maintaining the false belief that they're capable of stuff they aren't capable of (like truly caring) and 2) them maintaining as much as possible our delusion because it suits them well. It's a combination from hell, and it turns our world into just that: hell.

Rule for survival: "Neurotypical" and "narcissism" rhyme for a reason. (Well, it's a head rhyme.) Neurotypicals have a kind of group narcissistic obsession. Don't expect them to be genuinely interested in anything that surpasses their strictly human, neurotypical and personal experience.

HOLE TO FEED

"Oh can't you see, you belong to me?"
– The Police, Every Breath You Take

When a neurotypical uses the word 'love,' immediately translate it as 'desire' or 'attachment.' Things will then become a lot clearer.

Tiny mental bubbles simply can't accommodate something as big as love. Which doesn't prevent them from liberally spraying the word all over themselves and their tribes as if it's the only thing that drives them.

"Love hurts," they like to sing along. Well, it doesn't. *Desire* hurts, love doesn't. "Love is a battlefield" is another of their hymns. In reality, love isn't a battlefield. Desire, lust, and attachment definitely are.

While the real lover cries over the ill-being of a loved one, *they* cry over the non-fulfillment of their own desire. Both sadly mutter the name of the person in question, both may shed tears, but beneath the seemingly identical surface actually opposite processes are happening.

The main difference between love and desire is appropriation.

Someone who desires, wishes to *possess* the object of their desire. He or she wants this object always at his or her disposition, in a state and form that pleases them maximally.

Love, on the other hand, is devoid of appropriation. It's a deep, natural, instinctive drive for the loved one being well, happy, healthy, completely realized exactly in the way that suits them, not necessarily the lover. This implies also: free, uncaged, and not reduced to a playtoy, status symbol, fetish, or collection piece.

The only situation in which love is dangerous and destructive is when someone truly loving and caring starts a love relationship with someone narcissistic, psychopathic, sadistic, or otherwise toxic. The danger here isn't due to the nature of love, but to the nature of these toxic personalities. The latter are like black holes draining all the energy of the lover without ever reaching fulfillment or cure, and they may even find genuine pleasure in actively causing pain to the other (yes, some brains are simply wired like that). Often these toxic personalities engage in a long and destructive cat and mouse game where they draw the partner in with a mix of promises and superficial kindness, then start to hack away psychologically at their insecurities. When the victim tries to escape, they draw them back in with another mix of promises, false kindness, and overt or concealed threats. They hide poisonous attacks under what appears to be advice or just random remarks, convince their victims that they would be lost and worthless without them by their side, and/or play the victim themselves using emotional blackmail to keep the prey attached.

It's outside the scope of this book to delve into more detail about toxic personalities, but if you think you're in such a relationship, please inform yourself immediately on the topics of narcissism, toxic parents and partners, and psychopathy, and try to get out of their grip as soon as you can. Physically as soon as possible (like *right now*), mentally bit by bit afterwards.

Desire, on the other hand, *always* carries the seed of destruction. The main reason for this is that no desire can be truly fulfilled without destroying either the subject or the object of desire.

If the desire is temporarily fulfilled, it'll come back, each time stronger than the last, until it's so big, demanding so much to be fulfilled, that it cannot be safely fulfilled any longer. If it cannot be fulfilled, it's a constant source of pain and ill-being.

Desire is a normal and healthy function of the brain. But only if its nature is properly understood, and it's handled wisely, can it be part of life without causing destruction.

When the object of desire disappears from view, there is intense, selfish pain.

In contrast, when a loved person disappears from view, there's only the wish that he or she continues to be well.

In real human life, even true love relationships have a love component and a desire component. If a loved one dies, the *true love* part of the relationship will be able to handle this loss relatively wisely, especially if the loved one had a good life before dying, and there's no remorse of kind things not having been said or kind acts not having been done. At the end of a true love relationship nothing is lost, because there was no possession to begin with. Probably every human has desires too however, and this part of the relationship will cause intense pain and need a mourning process to take place for the pain to subside.

When two or more people truly *love* the same person, there's no conflict and no battle, because there's no appropriation. There's simply more caring and helping to go around.

When two or more people *desire* the same person however, there is only one of them that can appropriate the object of desire to the expense of the others. A battle takes place with only one winner. This winner then gets drawn into the quicksand of destruction described above. The losers are caught in the fire of non-fulfilled desire. And the object of desire gets appropriated by the winner. In the end, everyone loses. After a while the winner gets bored with the trophy and starts hunting for another one. Or the trophy can desire to be won by a 'better,' stronger party. Jealousy, treachery, and simply boredom are all waiting in line to spoil the precarious 'happiness' of the relationship rooted in desire.

In neurotypical relationships, the main component is desire, and love only enters to a small degree or not at all. If it were otherwise, most popular love songs would not be popular, but on the contrary be considered completely ridiculous, nonsensical, and ugly because of their selfish and appropriating descriptions of relationships. In many cases they're even quite disturbing. (See for instance the lyrics of "Every Breath You Take" by The Police, describing a creepy, controlling, and menacing obsession, rather than love. But even more generally, any variation on the line "you're mine" or "you belong to me" is already disturbingly possessive enough. And there's an almost endless list of "love" songs containing that one).

In itself none of this is a problem. It's not like neurotypicals can or should be 'cured' of their desire-based relationships. Their 'romantic' relationships are indeed battlefields, but so are many other aspects of their life, it's just how they tick. It's a direct and inevitable consequence of living in a small mental bubble. The real question is: do you want to be on the battlefield with them? Now you know the question and understand the mechanisms beneath the surface, *you* are the empowered one choosing.

Rule for survival #1: Boycott the battlefield. When a neurotypical talks of "love," translate it as "desire" and don't think he or she actually loves you, or ever will love you - not in the way you understand "love."

In fact, as a technical side note: "love" isn't the only word that has different meanings between neurotypicals and neurodivergents.

One could arguably define "the same meaning" as "causing the same (or very similar) neural firing." It's only logical then that brains that are different in form and function also give quite different meanings to almost every word and concept there is.

When I say or think "chair," this corresponds with a certain pattern of neural firing in my brain. This pattern depends on how my brain is wired, by "nurture" but also very much by "nature:" how connected the different parts of my brains are, which hormones intervene in what quantities, the relative and absolute sizes of the parts of my brain, et cetera. Between a neurotypical and a neurodivergent the neural firing patterns will be very different, even when it comes to a seemingly straightforward concept as "chair" - let alone ephemeral concepts like "love."

In the end, it boils down to living in different realities, which explains a lot of our day-to-day frustrations, misunderstandings and mistakes. But because we presuppose that the person in front of us has a similar neural firing than us when they think of "chair" or "love," and because it's practically impossible to always thoroughly verify whether this is actually the case, we often don't even realize to what extent we were actually discussing completely different realities. We gladly part ways thinking we had a good discussion on a subject, while we actually thoroughly misunderstood each other.

Rule for survival #2: Heed the homonyms. Words may

sound the same coming from your mouth or theirs, but the meaning is *always* different - sometimes slightly, but more often than you'd think, dramatically. Don't just presuppose that someone else, and especially not a neurotypical, gives the same meaning to a word or concept as you, even if, or *especially* if, it concerns concepts that are deemed universal like "love."

IF IT'S NOT THERE, IT CAN'T DRIVE THEIR BEHAVIOR!

Picture the neurotypical in their small mental bubble, happily scouring the Earth. The bubble isn't much bigger than their body, and whatever remains outside the bubble, also plunges outside their consideration. They may look at it, but they don't see it. They may hear it, but they don't really listen to it, and even less process it. They already have enough work with a few items to juggle, like their car, their pecs or boobs, their new fashionable handbag and that nasty bitch of a neighbor that just slighted them. There's no cognitive room to handle more.

Now picture various neurotypicals, lots of them, each in their own bubble, scouring the Earth, and bumping into each other. The bubbles are permeable, so they can overlap. Sometimes two or more of them come close enough to find one another partially within their respective bubbles. Lo and behold, an encounter of the third kind has just taken place!

Picture now the rest of the stage, filled with animals, plants, objects, et cetera. When these happen to enter the bubble, maybe in real life, or perhaps as a representation in a publicity, they waltz into the consideration of our neurotypical subject and possibly become the object of their desire.

Let's say a neurotypical passes by a shop window and a pair of boots enters their mental bubble. It's so unbearably fashionable it makes them want to scream. But what's *not* in their bubble is the child laborer in China who works 12 hours a day, 7 days a week, for almost nothing, producing these boots. Nor is the contamination of rivers and lakes caused by the production process; the sickness and death resulted from this contamination, now and in the future, of animals, plants and humans close by and far away in space and in time. They already have the object itself on their mind, and their mental bubble is filled to the brim with their own desires and projections of how exultant they will feel showing it off to their allies and enemies. They can't juggle anything else at the same time.

If you come along and try to push this object and this desire from their mind, and in its place install for instance an environmental or social concern, they'll reject it immediately. They'll even reject the simple observation that their feet will hurt because the boots are an orthopedic nightmare. Of course they will! What did you expect? There's only room for so much in their mental bubble; and instead of the pleasing idea of walking around in fancy boots and leave everyone jealous, admiring, drooling and gaping, you want to insert concern, guilt, and practical complications? Why on Earth would they cooperate with that? Especially because those who would benefit (like the child laborers in China, the animals in danger of extinction, and even their own actual, real-world health) aren't inside their mental bubble. They literally don't exist, from their point of view. How and why could they possibly be motivated by these concerns, or even want to consider them to begin with? It's asking the impossible: their brain isn't wired for it.

This is obviously a simplified description, but it functions well as a baseline. The point is that something that isn't included in one's mental bubble, in one's field of perception or thought, cannot possibly drive a behavior.

Once you truly, deeply realize that the neurotypical's indifference, lack of concern for justice and environmental protection, and apathy about the prevention of avoidable diseases and predictable mishaps, are simply the logical consequences of their *mental nearsightedness*, your outlook on them and on life on this planet completely changes. (If it doesn't, just keep the basic fact in mind as you move along your daily life, and bit by bit, experience by experience, over time it will. Guaranteed.)

To start with, you can finally stop being consumed by anger about their indifference and (what you think is) meanness. After all, you're not exactly *angry* with mosquitos for existing as they do, or with the rain for falling when it does. I mean, it can be annoying, but there's no sense in maintaining a personal grudge against mosquitos or rain, right? In the same way, it's completely senseless to maintain a grudge against neurotypicals for being as they are. Actually, once you understand how they are, how different they are from you, and that it's just nature at play, you can start *handling* them instead of nourishing the fires of resentment in which finally only *you* burn.

You don't handle rain by shaking your fist against it, or dragging a grudge along. No, you buy an umbrella and a raincoat, you learn to enjoy how it feels on your face, you stay inside when you don't feel like getting wet, you look at the weather report and plan your next day taking the possible reality of rain into account.

Once a reality is accepted, there are countless ways to handle it. You become the one in control. This doesn't only apply to rain, but also to neurotypicals.

Rule for survival: No cause, no effect. No engine, no locomotion. Realize that things that aren't part of a neurotypical's mental world, cannot possibly drive their behavior. Also embrace that their mental world is limited in size, and that whatever is not *fun* or promises some immediate, personal gain, has little to no chance of making it into their head, and even less of staying there. Actually, if your mental world were as small as theirs, you'd act exactly like them. So go with the flow, take their *mental nearsightedness* into account, be prepared and don't expect the impossible, and things will work out perfectly.

No FUTURE (HANDLE *WITHOUT* CARE)

The mental bubble of neurotypicals is very limited not only in space, but also in time, especially as far as extrapolation toward the future goes.

Concerning the past, they may have an okay capacity for memories, although one has to add that they don't seem to really *learn* a lot from the past (theirs or anyone else's). The actual *processing* of their past experiences and using them as a basis of extrapolation isn't really their thing. Their memory kind of just sits there, getting faded and distorted over time, like the photographs in grandma's shoe box. From time to time they open it, smile or cry or get angry, and close it again without any further effects. Hence, history repeats itself.

Let's state the obvious: neurotypicals suck at extrapolating possible future branches of events. If they try, the result is not a glorious, intricately ramified, complex tree of possibilities, probabilities, causes and effects, but rather something comparable to a short, thick stick. Or more precisely, a small club, with which they begin beating each other over the head. To make things worse, their tiny, stubby extrapolation is not based on facts or observations, but almost exclusively on their own desires and superstitions (see also the chapter above on magical thinking). Given the importance they attach to social status, they won't admit however that their tiny wooden club is only that. On the contrary, they'll try to make it come off as a glorious baobab of geniality.

So whenever they contend, "You think too much" (or some other variation in their extensive library of inanities), you can safely translate as "I'm actually too dumb to follow your extrapolations, but there's no way in hell that I'm going to admit it - not even to myself".

Now if you haven't incorporated the reality of neurodiversity in your worldview, and more precisely the fact that their brains are biologically incapable of certain things that for you are simple and natural; and if you haven't stopped self-projecting (unconsciously thinking that they're basically the same as you), then these repeated "you think too much" treatments by them can be devastating to your self-image. You'll probably end up extremely confused, torn apart between despising *yourself* for being the failure they make you out to be, and loathing *them* for being the obnoxious primates they are. Even worse, you might start to hate yourself for hating them, since supposedly it's not nice to hate people (while in reality, it's just a simple, biological repulsion mechanism at work). In the end, it's a kind of hangman's noose they prepare for you, in which you add your own head and then kick away the support under your feet, suffocating every day a little more.

The first, direct kind of self-hate is the result of actually believing the negative inanities they spew about you. You (very wrongly) presuppose that if enough people say the same, they must be somehow right. Well, they're not right about you, that much is certain. They're wrong about most things, in fact, but that's maybe somewhat beside the point here.

In the second, indirect kind of self-loathing you hate yourself for hating them. You *want* to be a nice person who despises nobody, but just can't avoid being repulsed by them. You then attribute this repulsion to some horrendous character trait of yours, while it's actually just nature at play. For someone with your neurobiology, their traits are simply repulsive and there's nothing wrong with that. It's like cats and dogs, or Diet Coke and Mentos: not a good combination. As long as you're not out to exterminate them for it, there's nothing wrong with not liking them (which at times gets so intense it becomes an understandable hate and loathing - still nothing wrong with that, it's just an emotion). But since you're unconsciously convinced that "not liking someone" is a horrendous character trait, you end up hating yourself for being a bad person.

Both forms of self-hate devour you from the inside out, and both stem from the same roots we have already discussed before: your not seeing the reality of neurodiversity, and your self-projecting your own characteristics on people who are significantly different.

So, to return to the main theme here, the neurotypical brain is terrible at extrapolating toward the future, but this isn't really a problem in itself. Lots of life forms don't extrapolate very well, like amoeba, ants, rhinoceros, pandas and ferns. That doesn't make them any less valuable or marvelous. The problem occurs when we, neurodivergents, think and act *as if* they *can* extrapolate, while in reality they can't. Based on that misconception, we put stuff in their hands that they can't handle in any responsible way. When the inevitable disasters then occur, we're flabbergasted or feel betrayed. All this misery happens just because we projected capabilities in them, that simply aren't there.

Neurotypicals today are liberally using machines, technologies, chemical substances and synthetic materials they could never have invented or created. They handle them gleefully and enthusiastically, but *without* care. Not because they *could* be careful and *choose* not to be so, but because they're simply incapable of extrapolating far and precisely enough. How could they possibly handle them with care if they cannot really understand what these things actually are and how they function (here it's important how one defines 'really' of course)? We put elephants in porcelain shops thinking they're delicate porcelain artists, and then wonder how it's possible that so much gets broken. The elephant is in no way inferior to the porcelain artist as a living being. But it has very different characteristics and these need to be taken into account - if we want to have some porcelain stuff intact at the end of the day.

Punk bands have sung (or rather yelled) "no future," and for neurotypicals this is very much true. Not because they *could* have had one and screwed it up, but because their dimension of future is so terribly flimsy and minuscule, relatively speaking, that for all practical purposes it equates to almost nothing.

The consequences of this are immense. All the song and dance to sensitize them into adopting a more sustainable behavior for instance, is of course to no avail (in case you hadn't noticed). They just check what the immediate advantage could be for themselves. If there's one, they'll swallow that advantageous aspect and spit out the rest. If not, they won't even touch it. Eradicating poverty or educating them won't solve the problem. This is proven by the hordes of financially well-to-do and highly educated neurotypicals that act just as irresponsibly, or much worse, as the poor and uneducated. Although, if that puts them in a positive spotlight, neurotypicals will swear on their mother's grave that sustainability is what they live and die for, and that it's everybody else's fault but not theirs if ecosystems all over the planet are constantly at risk of dying. Politicians point to citizens and citizens to politicians, consumers to companies, and companies to consumers.

Rule for survival: "No future"?

For neurotypicals, there isn't indeed. The future isn't an integral part of their mental bubble in any significant way.

For us, neurodivergents, it depends wholly on us. If we continue to take neurotypicals for what they are *not*, the future does seem bleak. If we stop projecting our own characteristics onto them and start seeing them as they really are, without overestimating their very limited power of extrapolation, a bright and shining future awaits us all.

A NEUROTYPICAL'S HOME IS THEIR UNIVERSE.

There's a saying that some people first consider the world, then their continent, then their country, and so on, to arrive lastly at themselves; while inversely other people first think of themselves, then their family and friends, then their neighborhood, and so on, and lastly the world. It turns out neurotypicals are ... neither.

They definitely first think of themselves, then of their family and allies. And there it stops. They never even get to anything bigger. You may think they consider their country, since they're rather big on flags, but that's only in appearance. They don't think of the country in terms of the good of everyone living there, they consider the country in terms of how it would be best *for them and their allies* (nothing more) in the (for them) foreseeable future (like half a day ahead, roughly). So they might have their mouths full of national concerns and ideas about their country, in the end it boils down again to "me and my gang, today." And if we're talking about *global* concerns, spanning the planet above and beyond nations, well, we might as well immediately stop talking - that's even less of a concern, or even a topic for them.

Again, this has far-reaching consequences on what to expect and certainly not expect from them, so in this respect we neurodivergents tend to make mistakes literally the size of our planet. We passionately put global issues on the table and discuss them vigorously and earnestly, treating them truly as global, in the sense that we take into account the whole globe and every lifeform on it. And seeing that our neurotypical conversation partners nod and respond with a comparable vocabulary, we assume that they're in the same frame of mind.

The question is: are they really? Instead of being on the same, global wavelength as us, our neurotypical conversation partners may simply be thinking, "What's in it for me and my gang?" They'd never confess this out loud, of course.

Are they thinking globally and selflessly, but systematically and inexplicably failing to follow-up with the logically corresponding behavior? Or do we need to see things differently, and accept the fact that they never even *really* considered the bigger picture to begin with?

In any case, when finally, in the days, weeks, and years to come, we're flabbergasted to see that they *act* selfishly and shortsightedly, happily shredding the planet to pieces in the process (using tools and concepts we invented and gave them, to make things worse), we tend to become very mad or very depressed. We then either get our hopes back together and start all over again making the same mistakes, or we give the world the finger and hide ourselves under our blanket (where they inevitably find us anyway and everything starts all over again, too).

Or, if we have read this book and learned anything from it, we say to ourselves: "OK, get with the program: they're not like me even if they appear to be, so let's take this reality into consideration and start from here." And we proceed to treat them as *they are*, not better nor worse than ourselves but definitely *different*. Integrating into the equation the exact characteristics they have, we instantly multiply our efficiency at what we want to realize in the world. We become all the happier for it, and the world becomes a better place.

Rule for survival: Don't forget that for neurotypicals, the credo is "Me and my gang, today." Everything that appears bigger, coming from them, is simply that: an appearance.

DID YOU SAY "SOCIETY?" (DROPS ON THE FLOOR IN A FIT OF LAUGHTER)

Society this, society that. Politicians, sociologists, psychologists, philosophers, moralists, journalists, your neighbor's uncle, his grandma and her parrot, they all have their mouths full of 'society.'

I have some important news to share, but first sit down, please, it may come as a bit of a shock. Are you ready? Here it comes. *This society that everyone talks about? It doesn't exist!*

Society, according to the Cambridge dictionary, is supposed to be "a large group of people who live together in an organized way, making decisions about how to do things and sharing the work that needs to be done"[4]. Well, *that* society doesn't exist. Not among neurotypicals at least. Happy awakening and welcome to the real world!

Remember our basic understanding of the neurotypical mind and the tight limits of their mental bubble? If one were to make a computerized model of a 'society' of such individuals, one would throw an enormous quantity of small spheres in a digital space and program them in such a way that each sphere would perceive only what comes into its own volume: a tiny fraction of the world, containing only "me and my tribe." If we were to let the program run and make these spheres interact, you'd have ... a bumper car attraction, not a society. Oh, wait a minute, isn't that exactly what our so-called 'society' actually is, if you look closely? Well, that's because to have a real society, every individual needs to take into consideration *all* the others. (That's a must, but it's not even enough by the way. A real society takes even more than that, like mutual caring, and a minimal threshold of fluid intelligence.)

Now if we'd make such a model with only neurodivergents with very large mental bubbles, we'd indeed obtain something like a society. I illustrated this in the diagram below. Each dot represents an individual, and around two of the individuals (the black dots) I've drawn a circle that represents their mental bubbles. Imagine if all the individuals (dots) in the drawing all have the same size of mental bubble (circle) as the two shown, then every individual would take into account all others. So as you can see, with individuals with large mental bubbles, we indeed would have something we can call a society. Everyone would take into account, in all of their thoughts and decisions, everyone else.

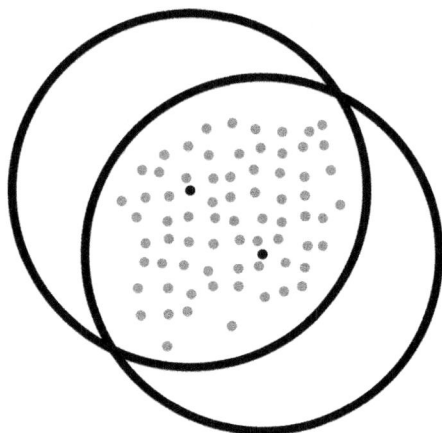

In the world of neurotypicals, the image is completely different however. I drew a representation below, zooming in a bit. Again, every dot is an individual, and around seven dots I drew their mental bubble, neurotypical size. In their small mental bubbles, they only take into account themselves, and at most a few others.

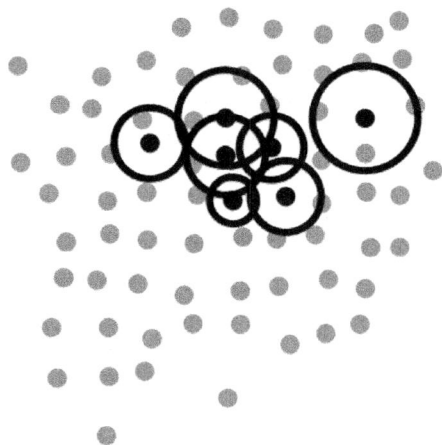

If we imagine these bubbles moving around, bumping into each other, each one driven by their own personal desires, attractions, and repulsions, from a zoom-out point of view we would see a lot of interaction, and probably a lot of patterns also - but not a real society. It might look like one, but it isn't one.

Some of these patterns would be like waves of movements toward or away from a certain stimulus. If you didn't know better, you'd almost mistake it for a group feeling, a society. But these waves would be caused by the existential similarities between the individuals in the wave, without there being a real society. Given that neurotypicals are attracted and repulsed by roughly the same stimuli, one can expect that they would all, individually, move toward or away from a certain stimulus as it enters the field. Like when you throw a banana in a cage of chimps, they'll all rush toward it. Throw a tiger in there, and they'll all rush away. Does this have to do with "a large group of individuals who live together in an organized way, making decisions about how to do things and sharing the work that needs to be done?" No. They all just go berserk and rush for the banana, or away from the tiger. But from a helicopter view, you'd see a seemingly organized movement and might think it's a society. Big mistake.

Another type of seemingly coordinated movements is caused by the typical herd-like behavior that for instance herbivores display: when a few individuals start running, most others, even if they haven't seen or understood the original danger themselves, just flee along with the few others in their sight. Does *this* have to do with "a large group of individuals who live together in an organized way, making decisions about how to do things and sharing the work that needs to be done"? No. They all just notice that the two or three individuals next to them start running, and blindly do the same. But again, from a helicopter view, you would see a seemingly organized movement of flight as a group. Big mistake again.

So how's neurotypical 'society' organized? Quite frankly, it isn't.

When was the last time you saw each and every member of 'society' come together and discuss at length an issue at hand, until they all agreed and then, in an organized manner, all proceeded to incarnate that decision in every thought and action, earnestly and responsibly? This is called participative democracy, and it doesn't exist in real life, except maybe at times in very small groups of neurodivergent 'alternative' people.

What neurotypicals do have is a roughly pyramid-like structure of chaotic power, defined by struggles, tit-for-tat, grooming, Machiavellism, rampant egotism ("me and my tribe"), small and large scale abuse, fraud and the occasional altruistic act (the latter preferably with a maximum of spectators so it pays off after all). But it's not even a pyramid. Because the president, even though he's supposed to be at the top, gets f*cked over by his car mechanic way below him who sells him unnecessary repairs at a multiple of the true cost, abusing the president's lack of technical knowledge. Meanwhile the mechanic gets f*cked over by the president in terms of taxes. The dentist f*cks them both over, abusing their lack of knowledge on teeth. And maybe the mechanic helps the dentist because he likes to have a dentist in his network of favors, but he might be having a secret affair with the dentist's wife.

The president doesn't really have the highest power in the country, because he or she needs to dance according to the tune of big money. But the big money people get f*cked over by their accountants who steal from them (or is it actually the other way round? or both?) and by their doctors who prescribe them unnecessary or downright unhealthy treatments so they can earn a bonus with the pharmaceutical company. And so on and so forth. *You* can call this a society if you like, *I* don't.

Compare the concept of 'society' to an ocean and the drops of water in it. When neurotypicals use the word, they refer to an effect on their own droplet and the few droplets of immediate interest to them. Actually, for them, as a droplet, whether they sit in a container the size of a tequila shot glass, or in an ocean, it makes no difference, they don't see further than the few droplets around them anyway. Neurodivergents with a large mental bubble on the other hand actually refer to the existential experience of the droplets in the ocean - *all* of them - *and* to the movements of the waves, the temperature gradients in the water, the large currents, and the consequences of all these, on every individual droplet, on the ocean as a whole, and even on what surrounds the ocean. Definitely not the same thing, but frequently the same word is used to refer to both: 'society.'

So if someone rambles on about 'society,' and includes primarily neurotypicals (as they usually do), you could very well ask: "What on *Earth* do you think you are talking about? As if these people have a mental horizon that's large enough to include enough others to even start speaking of a 'society'?"

I'd advise you to hold the thought to yourself, while you nod with an amiable smile on your face, before you excuse yourself and walk away from the nonsensical and slightly psychotic mind before you.

In the same way, it's completely nonsensical to try to talk social sense into neurotypicals, a complete and ridiculous waste of time. There you are, blabbering on about how 'society' should be, and what 'society' should do, while the neurotypicals in front of you are simply thinking "My God how boring" / "Hm, how could I use this blabbering to my advantage?" / "Look at his/her shoes, they're so out of fashion" / "Nice tits / great pecs / ..." / "Oh, I know just the remark that'll make me look smart here" / (complete with your own examples).

Rule for survival: the neurotypical "society"? Hahahahaha. Really. That's a good one!

SOCIAL CAPITALISTS

Given that there's no such thing as a neurotypical 'society' (see above), it may seem paradoxical to observe that neurotypicals invest enormous amounts of time, energy and resources in creating, maintaining and expanding their 'social' capital. So-called friends, allies, family ties, 'good' neighbors, they're obsessed with them.

The explanation is simple. The more positive relations they have, the more leverage they have when necessary, so the more personal advantage. A large 'social' network is very important to them considering that they're typically not very good at a diverse range of skills. They're either good at nothing specifically (apart from being annoying neurotypicals), or they have one or two mediocre skills at most which they developed with a lot of hard work and repetition. A neurotypical gardener will be only good at gardening, and maybe one or two other minor skills, but will be completely lost when it comes to health issues, finance, etc. And if they don't have an extensive social network that includes people with these skills, they know they'll be abused.

This is in sharp contrast with many neurodivergents who can be good at almost anything. They can easily learn new things from various fields of interest, and truly understand a wide variety of things. *And* they can inject what they understood in one subject matter into a completely different subject matter. These neurodivergents don't need to build up a social capital and obsess themselves with remaining on good terms with people with all kinds of skills, because they don't really need them to survive or live well. They can perfectly cope with most things themselves. So friendship can truly be pure friendship for a neurodivergent, while for a neurotypical there's always the aspect of social capitalism.

Apart from the practical need of having a phone book filled with as many "friends" as possible with as many different skills and power positions as possible, there are also psychological and emotional reasons for the neurotypical's social investments. Mutual gifts, helping each other out (not only in morally acceptable ways but also with fraudulent schemes and abuses, by the way), cajoling and grooming exist also because neurotypicals don't like to live with a lot of social tension. They know that other neurotypicals only tolerate them inasmuch as their own presence is of some advantage to them. They are always in danger of being excommunicated, which makes them *anxiously social*.

These two aspects together (obtaining leverage, and anxiety) result in neurotypicals being obsessed (at least from the viewpoint of most neurodivergents) with social capital.

This has some obvious effects, like their endless vocal grooming and chitchat, tribal behaviors, and hypocrisy.

There are also a few less obvious effects. Developing and maintaining their web of social relations takes a lot of time and cumulative effort. It's comparable to a gardener planting saplings, then pruning and fertilizing the growing trees, only to profit from the fruits later. The gardener won't just leave their orchard behind that cost them so much time and effort to build. In the same way, neurotypicals will not easily change their residence or their job, because this would mean losing years of social investment and having to start over again, socially speaking. They'd have to start building a whole new web of relations with neighbors, colleagues and friends starting from scratch. This also implies that if their friends, neighbors, or company are involved in fraud or crime, they won't easily turn their back on them, because this would also result in losing the social capital they have amassed over the years at considerable cost.

The net result is a behavior that is seemingly inconsistent with their own apparent values, because the *unspoken* top value on the list is personal advantage, and social capital as a means to obtain it. At the same time it makes them also quite inflexible, since they cling to their already amassed social capital.

Even being aware of this general characteristic of *social capitalism*, it's still difficult to predict their specific behavior in any particular situation. Just like the Wall Street stock exchange, the market of social capital is extremely chaotic.

This chaos exists partly because they themselves don't necessarily realize why they do what they do; and partly because, given the great deal of deception and hypocrisy going around among neurotypicals, and the difficulty even *they* have to detect lies, they simply make many mistakes.

As a result, they can be your BFF one day, or one year, or even years on end, only to drop you like a brick when your business value in their social capitalist bookkeeping wanes or inverses. When you become a social liability, things go downhill really fast. Or no-one is interested in you to begin with, which has nothing to do with you as a person, but simply because there's not much to be gained from maintaining ties with you.

While you're a promising student or career starter you may seem to have a lot of friends. They see in you a future power figure, and their friendship with you is like an investment in a startup that looks like it's going to become a huge money-maker later on. But if you don't deliver on that promise, through the years you'll see your circle of 'friends' dwindle to almost nothing, and you won't even know why because you'll still be the same friendly, intelligent, well-meaning person you always were. But there won't be enough fat to scrape off you, you'll be like a promising sapling that turned into a tree that doesn't yield enough fruit. And so no-one in the neurotypical world will notice your existence or maybe even tolerate your proximity.

Rule for survival: Don't mistake their investments in social capital with friendship. Friendship can truly be pure friendship for a neurodivergent, while for a neurotypical there's always the (big) aspect of social capitalism.

COOPERATION OF THE SLIME MOLD KIND

As mentioned above, neurotypicals aren't very good at a wide variety of things. This means they need alliances, and a lot of them. Because the car mechanic isn't good at plumbing, the plumber isn't good at accountancy, and the accountant doesn't understand anything about cars, they all need each other. Add to that the fact they're very materialistic, terrible at letting go (once they want that new car, they must have it or die trying), and extremely socially competitive (once the neighbors have a new car, they need one, too, and a bigger one at that), and you have a recipe for some pretty intense social ado. They'll also be well aware that if they don't find a 'friend' (read: ally) to do the work for them, they'll be cheated out of their money for an inferior product because that's how they operate themselves. In sum, in the neurotypical world, useful allies are literally worth their weight in gold.

Among neurotypicals this selfish and materialistic concept of 'friendship' is common but unspoken knowledge, and very acceptable as a situation. But you, as a neurodivergent, exist in another dimension, where social relationships are based on other foundations. Have you ever felt that you're an asocial weirdo with almost no friends, while they seem to be *so* sociable, having tons of great, close friends with whom they share truckloads of laughter, warmth and good times? That's because you're comparing apples and oranges (or more precisely, apples and durian fruit[5]). In reality, those 'convivial' neurotypicals are mainly doing stone cold business behind their fake smiles and enthusiastic outcries of social connectedness. Passing off as great, true friends is simply part of the PR.

It may also seem that they're very cooperative, and as far as the purely 'mechanical' definition of cooperation goes, they are. A piston and a spark plug of a car engine 'cooperate' in powering the vehicle, yes, but that doesn't make those mechanical parts especially imbued with empathy, friendliness, or a vibrant concern with each other's well-being. Cooperation is common among microbes[6], but it's not as if tender feelings permeate their togetherness either.

So it's important to unlink in our minds the concepts of cooperation on the one hand, and empathy, tenderness and being concerned with each other on the other hand. Cooperation in the neurotypical world is a business strategy, not an expression of something tender and warm. If we don't actively keep this in mind, we can easily fool ourselves into projecting much more empathy and human warmth on neurotypicals than they actually have.

Neurotypicals often band together to obtain a 'common goal,' but when you look more closely at the concept of a 'common goal' and realize how this concept can refer to completely different neurobiological and existential realities, things become very interesting.

For neurotypicals, a common goal is when person A has goal X, and person B has goal Y, and it so happens that X equals Y (which is not uncommon since neurotypicals by definition have very similar brains). They both have a personal goal, for which they have a purely personal drive, but by chance the content of their goals is the same. This can end in them competing, but also cooperating.

For me as a neurodivergent however, a truly common goal, and cooperation, imply not having boundaries between one's own goals and those of the other(s). From my helicopter view I see what needs to be done, where things need to move to, as a whole, for the benefit of the whole. I then check with how the others see things from their helicopter view. We then coordinate, and get the work done. (Note that for this to work, the others need to have a helicopter view too. Unfortunately, most neurotypicals don't have a mental helicopter license.) There isn't even a difference between personal goals and those of the others, but there exists only one goal, which is a group goal. This, to me, is 'real' cooperation, and existentially (and undoubtedly neurobiologically) it's totally different from the neurotypical form of cooperation. Superficially though, it may look the same: two or more people working towards the same objective.

Apart from having personal goals that happen to match, neurotypicals can also cooperate in situations where one individual needs the help of another and receives it, even if the second individual receives no immediate benefits from this cooperation. Technically speaking this is called altruism; but just like with cooperation, hold on a bit before you get all glowy and warm.

Altruism can regularly be observed in animals as small and simple as microbes. In Dictyostelium discoideum, a slime mold, solitary amoebae come together when faced with starvation, and some individuals die to form a stalk which others ride up to reach a better location to produce spores. But they're amoebae, unicellular organisms. They don't have a heart or brain, nor an Instagram account on which they view cute kittens and send selfies. And still, they can be perfectly and unmistakably altruistic. So altruism needn't go together with (human) emotions. You can literally be heartless and display altruistic behavior. This goes for amoebae, and for humans.

Experiments have been carried out where two monkeys, each in separate cages, had to pull together on a rope so that finally only one of them could reach some food. So one monkey ends up eating peanuts thanks to the cooperation, while the other one, who also cooperated, gets nothing out of it. The drive for this behavior could of course be 'real' cooperation as I defined it earlier, but not necessarily. It's much more probable that there is actually either a form of business going on ('I scratched your back so now you have a debt towards me which I can collect in the future'), or a form of fear and enslavement ('If you don't help me get my peanuts you'll be violently punished, now or in the future'). Monkeys have been observed to become violent towards non-cooperating monkeys. They also maintain an elaborate mental bookkeeping, being very aware of whom does favors to whom. And they hold grudges for long periods of time. Primatologist professor de Waal, in his book, *Chimpanzee Politics: Power and Sex Among Apes*[7], gives the example of a monkey who had been wronged by another monkey just before being separated in individual cages during winter. The first thing it did months later when both were released in the communal space again was to rush towards the wrongdoer and violently punish it. Put all these pieces of the puzzle together, and it's not at all improbable that monkeys cooperate simply to obtain favors in the future, or avoid possible punishment.

So, yes, neurotypicals do cooperate, a lot, but there's cooperation and *cooperation*. Again, just like with 'love', the meaning of seemingly universal concepts like 'cooperation' can differ fundamentally, although superficially this may be hard to detect.

Rule for survival: Check the cooperation, is it slimy or sincere? Detect the selfish altruists and the cooperative con men (and women). Don't be fooled by neurotypical displays of altruistic and cooperative behaviors. While your reasons for similar behavior may be selfless, their reasons can be quite different and not all that heartwarming if you look deeper into the matter.

THEY'RE TOO CHIMPANZEE TO BE TRUE!

"[T]wo chimpanzees were observed maltreating a chicken: One would extend some food to the fowl, encouraging it to approach; whereupon the other would thrust at it with a piece of wire it had concealed behind its back. The chicken would retreat but soon allow itself to approach once again - and be beaten once again. Here's a fine combination of behavior sometimes thought to be uniquely human: cooperation, planning a future course of action, deception, and cruelty."

– Carl Sagan, Dragons of Eden: Speculations on the Evolution of Human Intelligence

DIRTY POLITICS

In his seminal book *Chimpanzee Politics: Power and Sex Among Apes*[7], first published in 1982, the world-famous primatologist Frans de Waal states:

> *"The social organization of chimpanzees is almost too human to be true."*[8]
>
> – Frans de Waal, Chimpanzee Politics: Power and Sex Among Apes

Now, if two things are alike, they're alike, in both directions. So without doing violence to the meaning of the above quote, we can safely rephrase it as: "the social organization of humans is almost too chimpanzee to be true." (You can quote *me* on that.)

These primatologists have excellent observational skills and great expertise, and it would be foolish not to take into account the enormous similarities they describe between chimps and humans. But there's one extra thing to take into account: there are humans and humans. Neurodivergence. When they say "humans," they actually mean, without necessarily being aware of this, "The statistical mean of human", or "Your typical human." In other words... neurotypicals.

So let me rephrase prof. de Waal's quote again, but this time even more precisely, as follows:

> *"The social organization of neurotypicals is almost too chimpanzee to be true".*
>
> – Abel Abelson, How to Handle Neurotypicals

Now we're getting somewhere exciting. Because now we can use what we know about chimps and enrich our understanding of neurotypicals with it. But why would we use chimps to understand neurotypicals, instead of directly observing the latter?

Neurotypicals are really good at deception. (If you hadn't noticed, it's because they succeeded perfectly in deceiving you.) They use words like cloaks, smoke screens, sticks and stones to hide, confuse, attack, and defend. (Oh yes, and occasionally to actually pass on a meager bit of information too.) So they can easily confuse and deceive us as to the why, and even what, they're actually doing. And we're especially easy targets if we keep self-projecting our characteristics onto them, as explained before in the chapter titled "Me, myself and I (or how we create other people in our own image)".

Chimps, on the other hand, don't possess such developed language and conceptual skills. They don't go about explaining their behavior away. There's no facade of conceptual deceptions, justifications, and embellishments in front of their behavior and being. So in the chimp world, as primatologists themselves point out, we have a kind of mirror of human (read: neurotypical) society, a mirror that isn't masked by wordplay and conceptual twists.

The human-like characteristics of chimps go much, much further than the superficial behavioral quirks that so often make us laugh. In the preface of the same book, the zoologist Desmond Morris sums it up as follows: "*We are closer to our hairy relatives than was previously held to be possible. The apes, when carefully studied, reveal themselves to be adept at the subtle political manoeuvre. Their social life is full of take-overs, dominance networks, power struggles, alliances, divide-and-rule strategies, coalitions, arbitration, collective leadership, privileges, and bargaining.*"

I'll rephrase that for you, too, and add some of my own. You may think neurotypicals aren't very smart, and in many ways they aren't. Or more precisely, the tiny size of their mental bubble makes them terrible at foreseeing, extrapolating, and putting together lots of information from lots of dimensions and viewpoints. But don't be fooled.

Neurotypicals are extremely adept at the subtle political maneuver. Their social life is full of take-overs, dominance networks, power struggles, alliances, divide-and-rule strategies, coalitions, arbitrations, collective leadership, privileges and bargaining. And all of that's happening while they're chattering about the weather during a seemingly convivial barbecue. In fact, chattering about the weather *is* one of their many ways to conduct political maneuvers. *Almost everything is*, actually, for them.

Rule for survival: with neurotypicals, everything is political. They're not interested in facts, or the truth. They are interested in political effects. Don't be lulled by apparently innocent remarks or seemingly inconspicuous interactions. There's always, invariably, a political side to it, either in the back of their heads, or prominently just below the surface. Stay alert, and try to get what's going on in the social, hierarchical dimension. Something that may be of great help here is body language. It'd take us too far here to delve into this subject, but studying body language can give you invaluable clues about dominance, fear, subservience, and to a certain degree deception, also.

SELFLESSNESSLESS

Ever heard of "You scratch my back and I'll scratch yours"? The fancy word for this is 'reciprocity'.

It's no secret that reciprocity is one of the fundamental characteristics of human (read: neurotypical) social behavior. This has been recognized by ancient philosophers like Confucius[9], and confirmed by present day psychologists and anthropologists[10].

Interestingly, reciprocity is in no way unique to humans. It is in fact one of the basic principles of interaction between chimps. As primatologist Frans de Waal puts it: *"For the time being I would like to sum up as follows: chimpanzee group life is like a market in power, sex, affection, support, intolerance and hostility. The two basic rules are 'one good turn deserves another' and 'an eye for an eye, a tooth for a tooth.'"*[5]

I'll rephrase that again, so you can quote me on that one: *"For the time being I would like to sum up as follows:* **neurotypical** *group life is like a market in power, sex, affection, support, intolerance and hostility. The two basic rules are 'one good turn deserves another' and 'an eye for an eye, a tooth for a tooth.'"*

Reciprocity is often depicted as noble and heartwarming, an endless exchange of favors and niceness. But there is also a flip side to the coin: negative reciprocity. Backs can not only be scratched, but also stabbed. And a stab that's repaid with a stab is reciprocity at work, too.

Positive reciprocity is paying a favor with a favor in return. Negative reciprocity is paying back something unpleasant or negative with something equally unpleasant or negative. We commonly call negative reciprocity by the ugly name it deserves: vengeance. An eye for an eye, a tooth for a tooth, a deception for a deception, a disfiguration for a disfiguration, a life for a life. This also is reciprocity, and it's an integral part of the whole neurotypical reciprocity setting.

It's interesting to note that various studies have shown that positive reciprocity can be triggered by giving small favors (like a free taste sample). More importantly, the returned favor often tends to be bigger than the original one. This even works independently of whether the receiver actually liked the giver or not.[11]

Neurotypicals intuitively know this, and engage in 'giving' as a form of bribing, to start off a reciprocity that is designed to benefit themselves in the end. They give you something of little interest or effort to them, in order to maneuver you into an indebted situation with them. If you're even slightly more conscientious, more agreeable or more of a giving nature than they are (which isn't very difficult), they'll definitely gain from the reciprocity relation with you. Because in that case you'll make sure to give something back of equal or greater value (probably the latter, using a margin of safety). If additionally you're more selfless than them (which is even less difficult), you won't easily show disappointment, you'll be easily content, and you'll let unequal reciprocity in your disadvantage pass by without making a drama. From their side, they won't hesitate in pointing out (fairly or not) that they've been unequally dealt by you. In short, they gain while you, bit by bit, steadily lose.

Neuro*divergents* may offer things simply because they want the other person to be well, because they consider it fair to do so, because they're less materialistic and cling less to things, or because it benefits the situation as a whole to have the thing change hands, to name just a few non-neurotypical examples of true giving. But it's foolish and potentially self-destructive to assume that neurotypicals function even remotely in the same way. In reality, it's very rare for neurotypicals to give things for these selfless reasons. Genuine reports of selfless neurotypicals are roughly as rare as confirmed encounters with Bigfoot.

Rule for survival #1: "Thanks, I'm fine". If at all possible, don't accept gifts or favors. A neurotypical never gives anything truly for free (even if they themselves may be convinced of their complete selflessness at the moment). Avoid accepting favors if you can. In any case, it's standard neurotypical practice to pretend to not want to accept gifts, so there's nothing unusual about a *friendly* refusal of a gift. Just repeat, smiling along, that you're very fine as you are, thank them copiously for their generosity, and look for some pretext to go elsewhere or be occupied by something else. If the gift is truly in accordance with some previous service or gift of yours to them, they may be just trying to annul their debt and get back to zero, which is fine. In that case, accept the gift or service, thank them copiously again, and the reciprocity game can stop there.

Rule for survival #2: Instant karma. If you *must* accept a gift or favor, pay it back as soon as possible in a way of your choosing - and don't over- or underdo it, simply repay equally.

Let's say your printer jammed and you urgently need to print a form. You go see your neighbor, who is only too happy to oblige you (what's a piece of paper to them anyway, and for them it's a way of indebting you). They'll of course go through the obliged motions of assuring you they don't want anything in return, blah blah blah. But whether you like it or not, you're in their ledger now, in the juicy red column.

If you don't repay the debt on your initiative, one day they'll expect it from you on *their* initiative. Maybe they'll need someone to help haul their grandma's backbreaking piano from the attic and into a truck. So they get out their ledger, look up who's in debt, and who do they find? You. Their ledger says they have been 'kind' to you, so you'll have to be kind to them and break your back - or face the social consequences of being marked as unkind, asocial and ungrateful (which in the end isn't deadly either, but something you may or may not want to avoid). However, if the day after you used their printer, you gave them something equally small in return, say some apples from your apple tree, or some cookies you made, your debt is annulled also, and on your terms. Then, when it's time to haul grandma's piano, you have the social right to politely decline, because you're already even.

One final remark: don't give them something back that's exactly the same as the favor you received. The thing is, it must *look* like they don't want payback (although they desperately do) and you have to play your role well in this theater piece. If you repay your debt too literally, the business character of it all will be too painfully visible. They'll be offended because you show the truth of it all instead of pretending with them that it's all about pure kindness and selflessness. So instead of ostentatiously 'paying your debt', a few days later you 'casually' pass by and 'happen' to have some cookies for them, and let them revel in the opium clouds of their hypothetical kindness.

The negative side of all this, is that once you get into the reciprocity game, at every occasion it becomes harder to get out. The example above with the printing paper and the cookies would continue with an invitation to their barbecue (where you'll be bored stiff and/or silently freaking out), and then you'll have to invite them over, etcetera etcetera ad infinitum, which feels like being drawn into a puddle of quicksand or a gradually intensifying orgy of frantic back-scratching. Well, they call it 'having friends,' it all depends on your outlook on things.

I'd recommend being as autonomous as possible: on the one hand, by organizing as much as you can yourself, and on the other, by simply dropping whatever project you can't handle yourself (or with help of a few true, selfless friends - quality over quantity) unless it's absolutely critical.

VOCAL GROOMING

Let's kick this one off with Frans de Waal, our expert on chimps again: "*Chimpanzees are intelligent manipulators. Their ability is clear enough in the use of tools, but it is even more pronounced in the use of others as social instruments.*"[5]

Now this is a big one. Everybody has seen the image of two chimps plucking at each other's furs, right? Biologists call it grooming. Some of the main effects of grooming are warding off full-out conflict, and repairing social ties after a conflict does occur. (Fun fact: the more stressed out the grooming apes are, the closer they groom towards the anus. This is why you can see two male chimps who just had a rough fight and are now trying to make up, groom each other's anus regions where one is upside down on the other in a kind of standing 69 position. Somehow there's a connection with the neurotypical concept of ass licking, but we'll leave the details of that to some future Ph.D. dissertation.)

Grooming is what occupies most of a chimp's waking time, which should come as no surprise since a chimp, on average, also has several dozens of conflict situations to handle each day. If they'd violently fight out each conflict until one of the opponents is wounded or dies, they'd wipe each other out in no time. Or more precisely: those strains of primates that only fought and didn't groom, died out ages ago.

Grooming is a very complex occupation and should not be taken as something simple or insignificant by those interested in the social life of chimps or neurotypicals. It's where and when it all happens, and the way in which it happens, who grooms whom, in what order, when and how, all have far-reaching causes and consequences in a very entangled web of alliances and enmities, stress and relaxation, conflict prevention and conflict resolution, and so on.

Now keep the image of a group of grooming chimps in the back of your head, and mentally overlay it with a scene of small talk between neurotypicals. Picture the endless blabber about the weather, the wife, the dog and the lawn. Add some ooo-ing and aah-ing, some enthusiastic head nodding, a crappy joke, a fake smile and a head thrown back in a quick display of laughter. Top it off with a stealthy seductive look, a false little display of empathy and concern in passing, maybe a touch of the elbow and a prod or two. Oh, how you've been fooled until now by the apparent meaninglessness of these silly-looking, 'empty' encounters!

You have always correctly understood that a chit-chat session between neurotypicals is definitely not an exchange of information as such. They're not really organizing anything, they're not talking to inform each other, there's very little density to the data that is passed on up to the point of being outright meaningless. They state the obvious, ask the obvious, answer the obvious, fill the rest up with rhetorical questions, preprogrammed reactions, and trivialities. But the grave mistake neurodivergents make is that we consider these vocal exchanges as ridiculously watered-down and flawed versions of our own, information-packed, directly communicative way of talking. Our conversations are all about passing real data between two or more minds, concerning emotional, practical, scientific and many other profound aspects of life. If we use this as a reference point for understanding what neurotypicals are doing, that's missing the point completely, again due to self-projecting our own characteristics on these neurobiologically significantly different types of humans.

In fact, and you may be shocked by this, there's an *enormous* density in the information being passed on when neurotypicals chew the fat. There is real, very impacting social stuff being carried out right there and then. Only, the information isn't to be found semantically, in the content of the words and phrases. Nor is it to be retrieved from some sincere emotional expressions because there are almost none of those.

Between neurotypicals the real information is being exchanged in a kind of 'chimp dimension', by subtle and overt signs of dominance, fear, loyalty, disinterest, defiance and subordination. These are passed on through body language, but also through other aspects of social interaction like who addresses whom and whom not; who touches whom and how and in what order; who speaks first; who asks and who answers, and how short or long the answer is; how far or close one is to the other; in the tones of voices; etcetera. The semantic content is only a facade to be doing something entirely else. What it's really about is dominance, alliance, and enmity.

Actually, in ten seconds of chit-chat, two neurotypicals can set up a complete hierarchy, do their (conceptual) territorial pissings, declare dominance and possible war, or inversely (hopefully metaphorically) show their belly and piss on themselves in sycophantic submission; forge allegiances and set up enmities; and so much more. Businesses are started up, projects triggered or annulled, wars declared, brotherhoods forged, all in ten seconds of chewing the fat, a few glances and a body posture.

While we, neurodivergents, are wondering why on Earth they are talking about something as obvious as the current weather instead of occupying themselves with something more interesting or important, they have been occupying themselves with something more interesting and important, in *their* world that is, namely: their hierarchical power structures. They've sent out their tentacles from their small mental bubbles, sniffed each other's asses and groomed each other's butts, and maybe even threatened each other to (social) death. All in the space of ten seconds of what appears to be civil chit-chat about nothing. What you actually just witnessed during the neurotypical chit-chat is a whole tome of *War and Peace* by Tolstoy, compressed in ten seconds - and you completely missed it.

Yes, my neurodivergent friend, chit-chat is something extremely dense, and packed with breathtaking events, breaking news and shocking information (in their world, that is). It's like dogs sniffing each other's butts and the stale pee in the corner, only neurotypicals blabber on while doing so.

Rule for survival: Chewing the fat is a dense matter. Realize that their seemingly idle chit-chat and hypocritical, flimsy social encounters are, to them, action-packed chapters of an endless hierarchical battle. Then do what you need to do. If necessary, pay attention to the hierarchical going-ons just below the surface and use the data you glean. If you can, just let it happen and don't bother with it. This hierarchical cesspool isn't your world, it's theirs!

THE PRIMAL POWER PYRAMID

As I explained before in the chapter titled "Did you say "society?" (Drops on the floor in a fit of laughter)," there's no such thing as a neurotypical society. Yet they, and chimps alike, seemingly organize themselves in hierarchical structures. Companies, schools, sports teams, public and private organizations, even families and groups of friends, they all function in a hierarchical manner. Isn't that a form of social organization?

Well, the answer is: yes and no. Seen from the outside, it is. But raindrops also fall in an organized manner, all in the same direction, without the droplets 'organizing' themselves among each other. The fact that neurotypicals display a hierarchical organizational structure doesn't mean they all sat together, discussed at length how they were going to organize themselves, and then after much empathetic deliberation came to the conclusion that hierarchically would be the way to go, to finally consciously implement it together.

Reality is just a tiny bit more pragmatic. You only need two basic ingredients to form a hierarchical structure: endless conflicts and individual memory. Neurotypicals bump into each other, have a little (or big) fight, commit to memory who won, and next time, instead of risking being beaten again, the weaker one bows in submission or pees on him- or herself in advance. *Or*, if they feel lucky and powerful that day, they try to reverse the order and this time win, after which again both commit the outcome to memory.

This, in itself, is enough to end up very quickly with a hierarchical structure. No social awareness needed, just mindlessly bumping into each other, fighting it out, and remembering who came out strongest.

Neurotypicals are incessantly busy either reinforcing or defying this hierarchical superstructure. While it's true that *spectacular* hierarchical events happen only sporadically, like an emperor being deposed, a CEO being dismissed, or a team leader being replaced, these are only the tip of the iceberg, the culmination of a continuous process. These events were prepared for with copious amounts of chit-chat, vocal grooming, subtle instances of putting down or cajoling, and lots of Machiavellistic maneuvers long beforehand.

It's also important to realize that, in chimps and neurotypicals alike, Machiavellism (aka scheming) and alliances are the two main ingredients of moving up in the hierarchy, not pure, personal power (intellectual or muscular) as such. If you're smarter than your boss, and frustrated because you should be in his or her place, then consider alliances and scheming. If your boss is better than you at the latter, he or she doesn't need to be smarter than you. Among neurotypicals and chimps alike, those who manage alliances best come out on top, and they aren't the strongest or smartest ones per se.

Once you understand the neurotypical as a hierarchical animal[12], a lot of things become a lot clearer.

So much neurotypical shit that seems ridiculous, annoying or frustrating to us neurodivergents, is just a manifestation of this hierarchical fiber they possess, deeply ingrained in their being. I already mentioned the endless chit-chat, vocal grooming, and social fakery. But there's much more that finds its roots in this simple, biological reality of being a hierarchical animal. Think of war; capitalism; royalism; the eternal gap between the rich and the poor; celebrity culture; the giant success of competitive sports and the obsessive identification with random sports teams; the profound need for social status symbols; and so much more. If the tenacious existence of some or all of these behaviors has flabbergasted you in the past, here's a possible key for you: for hierarchical animals, it's simply in their nature.

Is it a good or a bad thing for (most) humans to be hierarchical animals? Neither. It's just the way it is. What's bad, is not taking into account this reality. What's bad, or rather stupid (because it's a fight you cannot win) is trying to fight nature in its very essence. What's terrible, for them and for you, is taking neurotypicals for something they are *not*.

Rule for survival: Pyramid spotting! Neurotypicals are highly hierarchical animals and use Machiavellistic tactics to secure the best possible position in the power pyramid. They're incessantly occupied with this, even during insignificant looking moments. Every bit of communication or interaction is loaded with hierarchical content, and moderated by a hierarchical structure that may be invisible to the naive, neurodivergent onlooker. Be aware of this and use it to your advantage.

THEY'RE FULL OF SHIT!

THE LIZARD AND THE MONKEY

There's a saying "Actions speak louder than words." With neurotypicals that's an understatement. You can safely crank that up to: "Their actions speak, their words *don't*."

To make things worse, even their actions are often part of a deception scheme. Like seemingly generously, but ostentatiously chipping in "for the noble cause," where the real "noble cause" actually is: coming off as someone who chips in for noble causes.

Up until my late twenties, I used to be very confused about politics. To be honest, I was confused about everything neurotypical under the Sun (which is a lot). But everything changed the day I started looking at politician's *actions* and *completely* ignoring their words.

This in itself wasn't enough to lift the veil entirely (deeply integrating neurodiversity and kicking my self-projection habit was the other major part), but it did rip a nice big tear in it. Through the tear a world started to show itself that actually could make sense, believe it or not. Especially when I began to apply to *everybody* my strategy of ignoring words and only taking into accounts actions. Yes, everybody, including my parents, siblings, colleagues, neighbors, and people who assured me with their words, but not their actions, that they were defending the same causes as I was.

It all began to dawn on me when I came across the website of an independent member of parliament, who had made the effort to list, for every vote that was passed, which party had voted in favor and which had voted against. I never thanked the man for it, which I now find a pity, because as humble and simple as his website was, the fact that he published and maintained it, definitely changed my life.

After clicking through the pages of his website, I was shocked and shocked again. The environmentalist party, publicly shouting from the rooftops how evil nuclear technology was, voted against a proposition to dismantle a nuclear weapons depot. The socialist party voted squarely against socialist measures, and the list of inconsistencies went on and on. (The independent member of parliament who hosted the website soon thereafter quit politics entirely by the way, outraged and disgusted, which is what anyone in their right mind probably does. Which in turn explains why so few people in their right minds stay in politics, and why politics is such a cesspool.)

After the first, and second, and *n* following shocks had somewhat subsided, I got over my initial anger and sadness, and a great feeling of clarity came over me. "Okay, all right," I thought, "I can do something with this". At least it was real, and it started making sense. (I seem to be one of those rare creatures that prefer a difficult to swallow realization over a sugary lie or rosy hallucination any time).

Looking at actions and totally ignoring words is not a trick, it's a paradigm shift. Crudely put, it's seeing humans as mute monkeys who have a babbling lizard living in their mouths. The monkey is silently going about its day for all the valid, biological reasons of its own, while the lizard, like a hybrid between a sports commentator and a spin doctor, is giving live the best sounding explanation to everything its monkey host does, so that the latter comes off as intelligent, morally acceptable, ethical, empathic, strong, reasonable, etcetera.

So there the mute monkey is, pottering about, pursuing mainly food and sex just like any good monkey does, using the (neuro)typical mix of threat, aggression, grooming and deception, going through the waves of contentment ("opposite sex genitals or banana in reach"), anger ("someone just appropriated the genitals or banana right in front of my eyes"), fear ("oh no, I'm getting out of ass and bananas"), attraction ("ripe banana, great ass") and repulsion ("rotten banana, unappetizing ass") in rapid succession. In the meantime, the lizard in the mouth is constantly cooking up its complicated explanations, and when the mouth opens, that's what you hear.

For instance, when our monkey grabs a banana from a child and starts eating it while the kid starts crying, the lizard will *not* say "OK, that was mean, I just stole a banana from a kid and stuffed it in my big greedy mouth" (the lizard calls the monkey "I" by the way, which makes things very confusing). No, in the blink of an eye it'll come up with: "Well, it's obvious that the kid was constipated and shouldn't eat bananas, so I quickly helped it and took the banana away from it. Then, to make the banana completely disappear from its view so it wouldn't be tempted any longer, I hid it in my mouth and then accidentally swallowed it. And I'll have to look into the eye infection the poor kid has by the way, its eyes seem to be a bit watery at times. You would swear it's crying, right? But no, it's just the infection. Or maybe the constipation also. And..." (babbling continues, fade out the sound).

So the trick is to now completely ignore the lizard (in other words, what people *say*) and only look at what the monkey does (what people *do*). You hear it, but don't take it seriously. Just like you would hear, but not take seriously, what a patient in a psychiatric ward says who is convinced that he's Napoleon. You can listen to his far-fetched explanations of why he, the great Napoleon, is wearing a restraint jacket and bashing his head against a wall, you can nod and say "uh-huh, of course, your Majesty," you can even ask him what his opinions are on the Duke of Wellington if you have some time to kill, but you're not actually going to take any of it seriously of course. Well, now apply this mental posture in all your interactions with your neurotypical fellow human beings. Welcome to reality.

Rule of survival: focus on the monkey, completely ignore the lizard. Hear what the latter babbles about, and process it like you would process the ramblings of a certified mad person. For they either literally do not know what they are doing, or know it all too well and shamelessly (or even proudly) lie about it to your face.

Two things make it a challenge to maintain this practice: a) the lizard does tell the truth sometimes, so you can't just dismiss everything as an untruth and b) often it's so utterly convinced of its own lies that when you don't believe it, it's *genuinely* shocked and outraged by such an 'unjust' treatment by you. That's because people tend to honestly believe *not* what is the truth, but what makes them feel good at that instant - *totally independently* of what's really going on. If you're not fully aware of this, you'll probably end up doubting your own sanity. Rest assured, the insanity is theirs.

STICKS AND STONES TO BREAK YOUR BONES

Neurotypicals exchange copious amounts of nice falsities (or false niceties, whichever you prefer), the vocal equivalent of chimpanzees grooming. But this vocal grooming also has a nasty flip side: they can, and will, very often use words like sticks and stones to break your bones.

These seemingly opposite uses of words have the same root: both cajoling and verbal bullying are ways of using language as a tool to obtain a desired effect, rather than a way of communicating information. Desired effects can be: humiliating you, make you cry, make you depressed, make you doubt yourself, give them something, etcetera.

Most of us neurodivergents tend to weigh our words carefully and use them to describe our perceptions, ideas and emotions as accurately and completely as possible. Neurotypicals employ words as tools to either flatter or hurt - but only rarely to convey information as such. For us, neurodivergents, words are messengers of data between one brain and another. Neurotypicals, on the other hand, brandish words to manipulate social power structures, alliances and enmities; to lower or raise someone on the social ladder; to advance their own hierarchical schemes. We focus on the information content; they aim for the social effects.

The problem is that at the surface, it seems as if they're

communicating information too, just like us, which is extremely confusing. They may appear to be putting arguments pro or contra on the table in earnest, or to share an observation or idea for the sake of getting to the truth of things. In reality, most often they're just trying to look smart ("Look mom! I said something too in this smart conversation and there was even a three-syllable word in it"), or to be the person that has the last word, which is a sign of dominance in their world. No matter if their last word is embarrassingly stupid, it's still the last word, and so 'they win.' Or they may bring up something just to change topics if the conversation is not suiting them, or to utterly confuse you. Often they'll also just throw you a bone you'll have to chew on for a while (in your search for truth) simply in order to get rid of you.

If we're naive, we let ourselves get caught in their arguments and lose precious time and brain power by honestly taking into account whatever random, borrowed idea they throw at us.

Compare it with this. Imagine a biologist is walking in the jungle, and a chimp picks up the first branch it finds to throw at the biologist's face. Instead of taking this act for what it is (an attempt to smash his face in with whatever is at hand), the biologist proceeds to investigate every botanical detail of the branch as if his attacker wasn't a chimp trying to hit him, but a scientist showing him an interesting specimen of a plant species.

In the same way, we neurodivergents are often caught in extremely tiring and nonsensical debates where some neurotypical throws whatever comes to their mind at us, which we then meticulously consider from every angle, investigate, put into perspective and finally in all earnestness debunk, only to have them immediately throw another one at our face from the same collection of nonsense. In the end, when they're finally out of arguments (which in no way guarantees that they feel defeated, or even appear defeated to their pack of neurotypical fans), they finish the conversation with some popular and supposedly funny platitude, completely winning the public over and leaving us flabbergasted, exhausted, and incredulous at how we can at the same time be so completely right and so completely ignored and misunderstood.

In *our* (neurodivergent) experience of this encounter, we've been investigating arguments and counterarguments to arrive at a better understanding of a certain subject. In *their* neurotypical experience of the exact same event, there was an exchange of random blows in a mental boxing match, and since they threw the last punch (the final platitude) and the public cheered, they won the fight. What the encounter was about for us (the subject matter), they don't even really know or care about. For them, it was about *them*, all along, from the start to the finish: *their* hierarchical position, *their* image, *their* personal advantage, *their* popularity, *their* pride.

Rule for survival: Heed the hot air. Don't waste your time or energy on the information level of a discussion with a neurotypical. They're probably just trying to obtain an effect in their hierarchical world.

ENTER THE META DIMENSION

But it doesn't stop there. If something can in some way be abused, you can bet your life on it that some neurotypical has found a way to do so, and will enthusiastically rise to the occasion whenever it presents itself. And believe it or not, they can even use relevant and truthful arguments as abuses. How? By throwing them at exactly the right moment, at exactly the right angle.

This makes it crucial in discussions to ask yourself not only "is this really true?" or "Is this relevant?" but also, "yes, that may be true and seem relevant, but *why* did they say *exactly this, exactly now, in exactly that manner*?"

I'll give an example. In a difficult discussion with my neurotypical father about his hurtful behavior toward me, at some point he said: "*I* think that everyone should look at *their own* faults first," and then leaned confidently back.

Now at first sight this may sound like a simple truth and a piece of sound wisdom that's relevant to the discussion. As such, it might look like an honest attempt to advance the subject at hand. But if you look at it more closely, you suddenly discern more than one snake under the grass. By using this apparently innocent piece of wisdom *exactly at that moment,* my father a) turned the heat away from himself (since he implied that I should look at my faults and not his), b) all the while coming over as 'wise' himself, *and* c) suggested that I was morally inferior to him, because I dared to look critically into his behavior. If I had grabbed the bait, the effect would have been: a) I would have diverted from the subject, letting him escape from the hot seat, b) I would have felt bad about myself, while c) my father would have come off as wise to boot. How strangely convenient for dad. Having already honed my skills in meta-level discussions however, dad didn't get away with it. I thought to himself "Nice try, but no go, dad" and continued focusing on the real subject at hand: the actions and personality traits of my father. Needless to say we got nowhere, but at least, I didn't allow him to shrink me.

I call this layer of a discussion "the meta dimension." It's the level of zoom out where you don't focus on *what* is said, but *why* exactly something is said exactly at that moment, precisely in that manner.

Rule of survival: Not "what", but "why". In a discussion with a neurotypical, even if an argument is true, valid, and relevant, always ask yourself: "Yes, but why, to what effect, exactly this argument, at exactly this moment, in exactly this way?" If you can maintain an awareness of this "meta dimension" together with the usual awareness of the content, you'll find yourself a lot more stable and less prone to being manipulated in discussions. And you'll find out, to your abysmal shock and horror, how much abuse is going on in this meta dimension without you ever having been fully aware of it.

"I KNEW THAT"

Social status is the alpha and omega of a neurotypical's life, and publicly admitting "I don't know" or "I can't do this" is almost like a social suicide. You and I, neurodivergents, don't make such a fuss about it. We don't particularly enjoy shitting on other people's heads, so being high up on the ladder next to defecating alphas isn't exactly our idea of fun anyway. But for neurotypicals, it's a question of life and death. Lowering their social status means lowering their chances of being helped, of having sex, of having friends (which in reality aren't friends but allies, and no other neurotypical wants to be a loser's ally), of making money and fulfilling their megalomaniac materialistic desires.

So neurotypicals have developed numerous sly strategies for concealing their lack of skill, knowledge and understanding, ranging from the very obvious and ridiculous to the quite sophisticated. The sheer diversity and, in some cases, relative complexity of these strategies, are silent witnesses to how important it is for them to succeed in this deception.

In the obvious and ridiculous category, there's, for instance, the exclamation, "I knew that!," when you give the right answer after they gave the wrong one, or "I was just about to say that," or even "I was just trying to see if you knew it." Sigh.

In the more sophisticated versions, they typically hide their utter cluelessness behind a slightly exaggerated serious expression accompanied by the occasional "uh-huh" and some intermittent nodding, sweating it out until they can divert the conversation toward a subject that does allow them to pass off as reasonably smart.

The more bold and adventurous types tend to apply the obfuscation strategy. Thinking to themselves that attacking is the best defense, they try to blow their audience away with a range of (real or imagined) technical abbreviations or pseudo-smart references to obscure things no one can actually verify at that instant, and come off as smart and knowledgeable, although they actually just blabbered a mix of nonsense and half-truths.

Some simply talk rapidly, in an effort to appear snappy and fast thinking. However, upon closer inspection, there's a lot of speed but no density or real value to their contents.

Knowing each detail of every deception strategy of theirs isn't what counts here. Being aware of their deceptive nature, and of their powerful fear of lowering their social status, are much more important.

Again, the fact that they deceive isn't problematic in itself. It's even quite natural, and chimps, for instance, are always in for a sham too[13], to give an example outside the human realm. Chimps and neurotypicals alike have every right to exist exactly as they are, two-faced or not. The problem is us, neurodivergents, *letting ourselves be deceived*. We unconsciously project our own honesty and consciousness onto them, which makes us the perfect, gullible victims of their trickery. But no more of that. Thanks to what we've learned, it's now: we've project*ed* ourselves onto them, which *made* us the perfect victims.

As everywhere else in this book, I stress again the importance of taking full responsibility for anything that happens to us, instead of whining, bitching, blaming, and morally judging. (You're allowed to waste your time creating and ventilating moral judgments, but just be aware that it won't help you or anyone else in any significant way.) It's time to wake up to reality and learn to deal with it *as it is*, to handle it *as it is*, in other words: *empower ourselves* instead of complaining and fruitlessly trying to bitch and moan the Universe into a version that coincides with our rosy little dreams.

This being said, one cannot but notice the devastating effects of this continuous deception on every scale, from the humble home and kitchen level to the bigger medical and financial dimension, up to the gigantic levels of global industry, environment, economics and world politics. If every doctor, engineer, lumberjack, plumber, dentist, car mechanic, painter, philosopher, psychologist, activist, influencer, politician, neighbor, and colleague on the planet would simply say, "I don't know" or "I can't do this," whenever that's the case, an almost equal number of disasters, big and small, would be averted. "I don't know" is frequently the only correct answer, and as such the only one of value. Once the "I don't know" is acknowledged, everyone concerned can then move on to the next step, either further investigating and eventually solving the problem, or embracing that actually no-one knows, and take reasonable action based on that realization.

A perverse effect of this mania of deception of theirs, combined with our naivety, is that we sometimes think neurotypicals are much more evil or mean than they really are. It goes like this. We explain something important to a bunch of neurotypicals. They don't get one percent of it, but won't be caught dead admitting this. We walk away convinced that they got it. They then proceed to act like dimwits. We then get angry and frustrated because "they understood it very well" but "refuse to act accordingly". We couldn't be more mistaken: they aren't even mean; in reality, they just didn't get it and we never got *that*. So in the end, it's us who's acting dumb, not them. Metaphorically speaking, it's like putting machine guns in the hands of chimps, and then getting angry when they start shooting around like ... monkeys.

It's not easy being a neurodivergent, but neither is it easy being a neurotypical: on the one hand, neurotypicals move among packs of other neurotypicals who aren't overly empathetic, smart, or caring, and they have to deal with that all day long. Besides, there are these "pesky neurodivergents" (from their point of view) who incessantly condemn and expose the exact double-dealing and violent strategies that allow them to survive among neurotypicals.

So what are we, neurodivergents, to do with this mess?

Understand it. Understand that neurotypicals are as they are, just like ants and trees and bears exist as they do. It would theoretically be beneficial for all if we could reason with ants and trees and bears, but it doesn't occur to us to desire that, because we consider them unchangeable in their nature. In reality, neurotypicals are unchangeable in their nature too, and yes, that includes that they're quite good at, and inclined to deceiving. So what? Once we've integrated this knowledge, we can easily take it into account.

Rule for survival: Check yourself before you wreck yourself! Neurotypicals are a deceiving lot. Make sure that when dealing with them, your end of the bargain is secure and safe. Take your measures of precaution. If you can't, be aware that you're at risk and don't push your luck. If possible, don't even enter in contracts and bargains with them. Never believe them on merely their word, never presume they won't double-cross you, now or afterwards, and even though they can in all sincerity swear something on their mother's grave today, tomorrow is a new day in which they may deceive you anyway. Or not, who knows. Just take a nice, big margin of safety.

HYPOCRISY? OR FILE UNDER STUPIDITY?

Neurotypicals are definitely hypocritical, but not quite to the degree that one might think. That's because part of their apparent hypocrisy is actually a lack of intelligence. Does that distinction matter? Yes, it does. If we want to handle them better, we need to understand *precisely* what makes them tick.

Let me give an example of stupidity that's easily mistaken for hypocrisy. All year long neurotypicals laugh in my face or ignore me when I point out the carcinogenic effects of pesticides, fine dust, smoking, trans fats and the other sick joys that make up the bulk of their lives. But once a year, when the national "Together against Cancer" campaign kicks off, they all of a sudden become anti-cancer champions and participate ostentatiously in this charity action, running marathons (or a few hundred meters), smearing badges and slogans all over their social media profiles, organizing stuff at work, and what not. All of this actually does a lot less against cancer, or nothing at all, compared with abstaining from using pesticides and solvents, buying organic groceries, avoiding the production of fine dust by using public or clean transportation, and everything else I mentioned all year long.

Their cheap and narcissistic self-publicity once a year seems excruciatingly and unbearably hypocrite, especially in the light of their disdain for true solutions the rest of the year, and it partly is. But it's important to see that in reality something bigger and completely different is going on, too: a gigantic lack of intelligence. Which is arguably not better, but it's a whole different ball game. And if we want to come to terms with reality, and learn to handle neurotypicals efficiently and in the most agreeable way for all concerned, we'll have to get our observations in order.

Let me explain the stupidity part. Bear in mind that neurotypicals do want to remain fit and healthy, and are terrorized by the idea of cancer. Once they have the disease, they do everything to get rid of it, from doctor's visits to praying and whatever charlatan's remedy convinces them. So it's not as if they don't care about cancer. They do. Yet they *knowingly* (because I informed them) expose themselves to the causes of cancer all year long, and knowingly participate in creating these causes. This is not hypocrite. It's simply a lack of processing power.

If someone hits their finger repeatedly with a hammer, and it hurts, and they really do understand the link between the hammer and the pain, they will completely refuse to continue hitting their finger, even if you were to implore them. Not for the life of them will they continue hitting their finger, *understanding* that it'll cause more pain. It's not like they'll keep on hitting their fingers all year long, and only participate one day per year in a campaign against finger pain.

With the cancer example above, it's actually the same.

Only here, at a surface level, it becomes less clear, because a person may appear to have *understood* while they actually only *memorized* it. You can explain to a neurotypical the link between certain substances and cancer, and they may well be capable of repeating the explanation. We tend to be deceived into thinking that this means they actually got it. They haven't (as attested by their not putting their apparent understanding into practice). Only a few school or university exams actually test for deep understanding, so there are even a lot of graduate degree holders in the wild who did a lot of rote learning but never actually got it either. (As attested by their manifestly not putting into action what they supposedly understand.)

So the neurotypical doesn't *really* get it when you explain the link between carcinogenic substances and cancer. Otherwise, terrified as they are of getting cancer, they'd immediately and energetically refrain from using those dangerous substances all year long. (Remember the hammer and the finger pain). But here comes the interesting part: they won't admit to a lack of understanding - because, as explained earlier, that would lower them on their sacrosanct social ladder.

We neurodivergents tend to be flabbergasted, disgusted, and utterly frustrated because of the incongruity between their apparent understanding and their actions. I propose we change that and get real. Let's simply accept that they completely didn't get it and never will.

If you really do this, you'll notice that it actually starts a kind of mourning process in you. If they aren't able to understand *that*, then what else don't they understand, and what does that mean for the world, and how on Earth are we going to cope with all that stupidity? It's kind of devastating at first, if you truly delve into it. So most neurodivergents actually remain stuck in the negation phase of the mourning process and put great effort in trying to maintain their 'belief in humanity.' (And it's actually just that, a belief, with nothing real behind it.) But when you finally get through all the stages of the mourning process, you end up having personal peace, and a highly boosted efficiency, and *that's* where we want to end up.

So, in short, a lot of what we ascribe to hypocrisy, is simply stupidity.

Now I'm not denying there's a lot of plain, old-fashioned, undiluted hypocrisy going on. Like pretending to be happy with a completely failed Christmas present. Or pretending to like you, or find some crappy joke funny. Or a politician acting as if he never personally heard of the existence of fraud while the illegally gained dollar bills burst from every pocket in his expensive suit. Or two neighbors wishing each other the very best while they actually hate each other's guts but still prefer to keep their social bookkeeping on the plus side ("You never know when you need a friend", right?). There's *lots* of hypocrisy going down.

But if we ascribe *everything* to hypocrisy, even though a good part of it is simply a lack of intelligence, we'll be a) more frustrated than necessary; b) we won't be able to see what's really going on; and c) be madder than we should be at neurotypicals, because while hypocrisy may be a reasonable cause for anger, stupidity isn't. You can be angry at someone with perfect vision running into you as if you didn't exist. But being pissed at a blind person running into you just doesn't make sense. They really, honestly, simply couldn't help it.

(Let me repeat also that there's no problem whatsoever with low intelligence as such. It's a characteristic, and the people concerned are perfect as they are. It's a given that simply needs to be taken into account for everyone's sake.)

Rule for survival: Hanlon's razor to the rescue. "Don't attribute to malice that which is adequately explained by stupidity". A lot of what seems like hypocrisy on the part of neurotypicals is actually a result of (relatively) low intelligence and the incapacity to understand (relatively) complex issues, combined with the obsession to hide their personal limitations. Being angry at them for this, or resentful, makes no sense at all. It also means that they're less vindictive than we take them to be - and less intelligent also. See them for what they really are, accept them as they are, and act according to your observations.

WRAPPING THINGS UP: HOW TO HANDLE NEUROTYPICALS

So, we've learned a lot about *Homo neurotipicus*, this strangely normal animal that scours the Earth multiplying as if God herself ordained them to. How can we, neurodivergents, apply this newly found knowledge in our daily lives and empower ourselves?

Here are the Five Commandments for the Empowered Neurodivergent.

FIRST COMMANDMENT: GET WISE ON *HOMO NEUROTIPICUS*.

If you plunged into this book and dove right to this chapter, study the previous chapters on the characteristics of *Homo neurotipicus*. (I know you're impatient and want to get the bottom line first, that's what I always do too, but it'll all make so much more sense if you backtrack first.) Each chapter comes with a rule for survival to put your newly found knowledge to use. Study the descriptions, assess the rules, think about them, then put them into practice.

These aren't recipes; instead, they're a GPS to guide you on a journey. The destination is personal empowerment, peace of mind, and efficiency. The insights in the previous chapters are indispensable aids on your journey.

Along the way, add your own observations and continue your research until you can honestly reward yourself with a **Ph.D. in neurotipicology**. Only then will you be truly at ease, and truly empowered on this Planet of the Apes. Don't forget to have fun along the way!

SECOND COMMANDMENT: ACCEPT THIS PARTICULAR MAMMAL'S EXISTENCE *AS IS*.

If you look at it from a zoologist's point of view, *Homo neurotipicus* is first and foremost a hierarchical, competitive animal. They're also mentally nearsighted (the more polite way of saying 'selfish and somewhat stupid'), materialistic, deceiving, tribal, driven by social status and personal gain, and quite unaware of what's really going on in their own minds and bodies, let alone those of others.

Does that make them horrible? Not if you *know* that's how they are, accept it, and thus handle their existence with relative ease. They're less mentally nearsighted, materialistic and unaware than most other mammals. If you can embrace the existence of all those other mammals as a given, you can accept *Homo neurotipicus*'s existence, too.

We can honestly appreciate the existence of every animal, plant, and rock, just as it is, from poison ivy, spiders and hookworms to cute baby pandas, kittens and majestic sequoias, and everything in between. It's all part of Nature's wonders. But "appreciating their existence" doesn't necessarily mean "seeking out their proximity." I love volcano craters and glowing lava, but I stay at a safe distance from them. Polar bears are great, but not in my living room or even my town. It wouldn't benefit them, or me, to install myself with all my technology in the midst of their pristine natural habitat.

With neurotypicals, physical distance isn't even all that necessary. We can perfectly be close neighbors. But we're not meant to be Siamese twins. Applying everything we learned about them in the previous chapters, we'll no longer be taken by (unpleasant) surprise, or hope for the impossible. This will allow us to become great friends - *from a nice, clear distance*.

So the general mission here, for you (and I) as a neurodivergent, is the following: **accept them as a given**. Get off their backs with this obsession of changing them, be it individually or as a species. (It'll instantly relieve you of a lot of them who are on *your* back as a response to *you* being on *theirs*).

Focus on a change within, not out there. Not because I told you so, or because it sounds all wonderfully fluffy and spiritual. Do it because **it's a position that's so much more empowered**. Because it's realistic and mature. Because it's so much more fun. Because it'll be the end of your frustration, anger and disappointment. Because it's time to get on with your life and leave those @#!?& neurotypicals where they are. Live and let live!

THIRD COMMANDMENT: ALWAYS BE READY TO FIGHT.

If you take their three main characteristics together as outlined in the previous chapters, namely their mental nearsightedness, their 'chimpanzeeness' and what I called their 'being full of shit,' one general consequence of their existence on this planet stands out: **you need to be ready, willing, and able to fight**. They're not going to take you into account, they're always in for their own advantage, and they're deceiving as hell. You can't just live with them as if they're the most saintly empaths in the Universe. You'll have to actively stand your ground, and at times force your way.

Now by fighting I don't mean going out there, throwing yourself at them and beating the crap out of them. I mean like a martial artist, first and foremost figuratively speaking, but frankly, it does help to be one literally, too.

The true martial artist almost never gets into a fight. They exude readiness, willingness and ability to fight, so no-one picks a fight with them to begin with. Like any other animal, neurotypicals seek out the weak if they want to attack, and the mere prospect of a (metaphorical or physical) beating, especially in public (remember their sacrosanct social status) is enough to deter them. They're not evil, they're just indifferent and in for a quick win. If you truly incarnate empowerment and determination, they won't even come close to you. If someone does attack the martial artist, it doesn't become a long and dirty barroom fight, but a quick and efficient exchange to simply put things in their right place. (Like the martial artist's knee pinned on the back of the squirming attacker.)

So, you have to always be ready to fight with neurotypicals, because they're always ready to challenge, deceive or abuse you. You have to develop the skills, the awareness, the knowledge; you have to know how to turn a situation to your advantage and not let anything or anyone break down your mental or physical structure. And then... you'll only use one percent of those skills. Because it'll emanate from every pore of your being that you're not to be messed with, and as a consequence, they won't mess with you. That's the true power of the accomplished martial artist.

If you're ready to fight with them, they'll respect you. If

not, they'll take advantage of you. If you're ready to fight, you'll stand on equal mental grounds, and your dealings with them will be just and equitable - because you will force them to be so.

If you're ready to battle, you'll have peace. If not, they'll constantly besiege you, and get away with the loot. That's how it is on this planet, take it or leave it.

So, practically speaking, what do you need to do?

In most civilized countries and settings, physical fighting is not a real problem. You can quite easily avoid places where you're prone to be physically attacked, so I'm not going to say you absolutely need to develop physical fighting skills. However... Every human being has a civilized part to them, but also an animal part. By 'animal', I don't necessarily mean savage and violent. I mean a part, a dimension, that instinctively and beyond the reach of rationality reacts to and emits smells, pheromones, body language cues, et cetera. Most people envision themselves and others as if this animalistic dimension is suppressed by, or hidden beneath, the civilized part. It's not. They're there in parallel, fully present, and fully active at the same time. While your civilized part is thinking "yes, I quite agree with this line of reasoning," your animal part is 'thinking': "He smells like testosterone" or "That's a dominant position, I'd better shrink a bit before he/she attacks." And both sides, the civilized and the animalistic part, will influence each other, and your behavior as a whole.

This means that if your animalistic part is clearly weak and unskilled in even the most basic levels of physical conflict handling, you'll emanate this to the animalistic part of the person in front of you, and he or she will tend to dominate you and disrespect you. And this will spill over into the civilized part of the encounter. You may even preemptively avoid conflict at all cost, both physically but also in arguments and discussions, because your animalistic part will tell you: "don't push your luck, you're in physical danger."

Whether you actually are in physical danger or not, isn't the point. It may be true that your bullying manager won't actually throw himself on you and punch you. The point is that your brain is wired, through evolution, to sense the danger and react to it, and you can't just turn that off. Which is why I actually do recommend getting into some physical upgrading, and more precisely, to take up a martial art of your choice.

Martial arts are cool and fun. But on a more profound level, they'll develop your stability, both physically and mentally; they'll train your awareness and readiness to react; they'll confront you with your fears and uncertainties, your limits and untapped potential (again both physically and mentally). While you study your martial art and gradually become better at it, you'll see that things around you will change, even things that seem completely unrelated now. I'd almost say that *people* around you will change, but what's actually happening, is that they sense the change in you and react to the new you.

FOURTH COMMANDMENT: PURGE THE PROJECTING.

Another important thing to do is to **stop self-projecting** yourself on everyone (or at least to become aware of when you're doing it) - see the chapter on that for more details. Stop projecting, and start studying people, almost like an undercover zoologist in the field. The main thing to learn here is: **never forget that neurodiversity is a reality**. Most neurodivergents are so different from neurotypicals that it's almost like a different subspecies.

If the bonobo takes the chimp for a bonobo, it'll always be in for (mostly unpleasant) surprises. If it realizes that although the other looks like a bonobo, it behaves, thinks and feels very differently, its life will drastically change for the better.

FIFTH COMMANDMENT: KNOW THYSELF.

It sounds like a classic one, but for once, consider it in a very concrete, hands-on, real-life way: you have to get to know yourself. If you haven't seriously started doing this, you're spectacularly full of mistaken ideas and presuppositions about yourself. You're living a dream (and/or nightmare), right in the midst of reality, like a sleepwalker. If you don't think so, it's because you haven't even started this journey inward.

Getting to know yourself turns this life into an adventure instead of a confusing nightmare, a deadly boring theater piece or an endless, meaningless torture. I know meditating is a good way to do this, although you'll find that the world of meditation is filled to the brim with its own challenges (neurotypicals using it for social status, among others) - but that's part of the process. Other methods and practices may work for you, too, or even better. Whatever the practice or flavor, one thing to hold in mind is this: don't try to *change* yourself, try to *know* yourself. **Seriously study yourself, and have fun doing so.**

OR IN OTHER WORDS

"You are the mother-fucking shit

You are great, you are magnificent

You can do whatever you want to do in this world

Put your mind to it, put your grime to it

And you can do it!"

– Get Up Get Out, Born Dirty Featuring Jslbby

AFTERTHOUGHTS

SPECIAL CASES: HOW TO HANDLE...

NEUROTYPICAL PARENTS

"There's no need to argue. Parents just don't understand"

– DJ Jazzy Jeff & The Fresh Prince, "Parents Just Don't Understand"

If you're not neurotypical but your parents are, that's a tough spot to be in. They'll interpret every single one of your actions, reactions, ideas, dreams, questions, doubts, and decisions backwards.

While you're young, they'll tend to over-dominate you, being unnecessarily authoritarian and demanding while they could just ask like a friend and explain properly. (An added problem is of course that they're incapable of explaining properly because their brain doesn't process stuff the way you need them to process it.)

When you get older, they'll mistake reasonable questions and genuinely smart observations for defiance and disrespect. They'll try to maintain their cramped, dominant grip on you, not realizing they have actually already lost it because you outsmart them in many things. They'll take your 'weird' behavior, style and fields of interest for attempts to 'simply look special', while actually, well, you *are* special. They'll slap you over the head with advice that may or may not be fitting for neurotypicals, but that definitely is humbug or poison for you as a neurodivergent.

Then, when you're an adult and living on your own, they'll frown on how you meander through life, 'squandering' what they see as golden opportunities, 'wasting' your time and energy on stuff that's really important and satisfying to you, and tearing out their hair concerning the friends and partners you frequent. Or, much worse, they'll be so content and proud of the overadapted wretch you have become in order to please them, that they'll pat you on the back and praise you to the skies for your acquired neurotypical behavior, while on the inside you are dying every minute of your life.

It's hell on Earth.

But, there's hope.

As a child, before your teens, it's true that you'll have to accept the hand that life deals you. If you're lucky enough to have a neurodivergent grandparent, uncle or aunt, neighbor, teacher, older brother or sister, companion, or some other guardian angel that takes you under their wings, this kindred spirit will nourish you and you'll have an easier time. If not, it'll be like salmon swimming upstream. You'll make it, but not without some damage, which luckily can always be repaired later. Once you're a teen, you'll start having things more under your control. It'll be easier for you to choose who you frequent, and you'll have somewhat more practical liberty (if needed, hidden from your parents) concerning what you occupy yourself with.

I'm going to tell you something for which parents all over the world will want to kill me. But it's the only sound advice I can give. If your parents are neurotypical and you aren't, stop considering them as your parents. See them as people from another dimension, that tend to take a lot of space in your dimension, and you'll have to deal with that fact in some way, taking into account their characteristics as a given. Now hold on! Read on first! They won't understand this, and you definitely shouldn't try to explain it to them. Most important of all, don't shove this book under their noses to confront them with any of this, because they'll just throw it in the stove right then and there (and put a price on my head). You'll have to be the smart one of the three of you. If you have read all the previous chapters, you'll know all about their mental nearsightedness, their need for social status, et cetera. (If you haven't read those parts, do so now.) That's biology, it's not their choice. Don't ask your parents to understand any of this, or to understand you. They *can't*. Don't even secretly expect it from them. Don't even hope for it somewhere in the deepest, hidden crevices of your mind. Just like you don't ask, hope for, or expect from an elephant to fly.

So just play along on the surface. Play the son or daughter role, and neither under- nor overdo it. Make it as easy on yourself as you can. Don't exactly give the emperor what the emperor wants. Give the emperor the *idea* that they get what they want, but don't feel bad about hiding something here and there from them, as long as you do it intelligently and benevolently. Don't give them more of a hard time than necessary, because it'll simply fly back in your face. But don't comply more than necessary either. In your mind, make a kind of business deal out of it, like a contract. If it were a class, aim for a 5 out of 10. As a son or daughter, strive for a similar score. Good enough to not attract heat, but not that good that you sacrifice yourself more than necessary.

Divide your time and energy between a maximum of interesting and satisfying stuff for you, and the minimal necessary cooperation with them to make things go smoothly. In fact, if you play it right, your parents instead of putting a price on my head, might even want to thank me. Because a lot of the overt tension and ill-being will have dissipated, and both you and they will be the happier for it.

To fill the emotional and cognitive void that your neurotypical parents leave, seek out people like you, of any age, and make contact with them. That may be difficult, but it's vital that you try. Remember that many neurodivergents are heavily damaged by childhood trauma and life in general. Even if they're smart, they may be hiding in inconspicuous jobs (underachieving is widespread among neurodivergents) and under inconspicuous external personalities. There are not a lot of them out there, so don't be too picky. Brain compatibility is the key here. Age, occupation, social status, and style shouldn't interfere. Also, bear in mind that even if they're not neurotypical, they can and will have some (or many) differences with you. You'll have to find ways to deal with those. And don't look too far to begin with, they may be hiding in plain sight (just like you probably do).

I'd like to tell you otherwise, but the agony with neurotypical parents doesn't magically stop just because you become an adult. They remain neurotypicals and you remain neurodivergent, and your brains still won't match. They'll have the tendency to continue appropriating your life as part of their own social status, they'll fail to understand anything about you and thus disapprove of most of what you think, say, and do. But hey, the good news is that, at that point, you're an adult too, just like them. You're on equal footing. You don't depend on them for survival. So you're now completely free to relate yourself with them in any way necessary. If you have found the love of your life and they rigidly disapprove of him or her, well, screw them. If you want it to be so, they're two random people just like any other random people. You're totally free to not have any relationship with them whatsoever.

Now it doesn't have to be like that necessarily, but if you take it like that, you'll meet each other on equal terms, and they'll have very little grip on you to manipulate you or make your life difficult. Because if you realize you can say "screw you" to them anytime you need to do so, and if you allow yourself to do so if and when necessary, you're in a very strong position - and chances are you'll never have to tell them to get screwed. Because you can probably just be relatively nice to them, without groveling or seeking their approval, taking into account their specific (annoying) characteristics and limitations, which will probably be the easiest option for you. But you have my personal blessing to tell them to get screwed, too. To hell with the fifth commandment, or, if it needs to be kept, let's add an eleventh: "Honor your children." There's no need to remain in the shadow of your parents if they're a toxic influence in your life. Screw everything that's toxic, including if it happens to come from biological parents.

NEUROTYPICAL TEACHERS (SCHOOL DAZE)

Oh man, I don't know which is worse, neurotypical parents or neurotypical teachers. Neurotypical parents have more time and omnipresence to make your life miserable. Neurotypical teachers have a free pass to be sadistic power abusers and are paid to waste spectacular amounts of your precious life in the worst ways possible. To make things worse, parents and teachers band together in a kind of devilish pact to make your life a living hell of meaninglessness, boredom, suffering, and slavery, which they call "education."

Sigh.

If you have at least one neurodivergent parent who's really your friend, seriously consider homeschooling. If not, don't despair, since you can optimize the school experience. It'll never be heaven, but still, if you approach it wisely, you can avoid a lot of misery.

To begin with, don't bother with excellent grades. They're of no importance whatsoever. Once out of school, no one gives a hoot about them anyway. I've applied for quite a few jobs (I like changing jobs because it keeps life interesting), and never, ever, has anyone asked for my grades. It's like a taboo; it's not done. Experience, yes, diploma, yes, personality, a lot, proficiency in languages, a lot. But grades, not a peep.

Don't go for especially bad grades either and don't be excessively sloppy, because it'll also get you in trouble too. You don't want to spend even more time in school because you flunked, right? So, in all subjects that are of no particular interest to you, go for *mediocre*. That's right, aim for a 5 out of 10, or maybe a 6 or 7, so you have a small margin of safety. But don't waste your time in adding the last 30 or 40% to attain excellence. These last straws demand a disproportionate amount of effort (compared to just passing) and are completely worthless. Nobody will *really* like you any better for having ridiculously good grades, probably on the contrary. Teachers will use you as their pet, which will understandably make other students hate you. There's nothing whatsoever in it for you.

Excel only in subjects that are fun and interesting. It'll be easy and natural for you, and you'll earn the necessary respect with those alone. It'll further show that you're not a dimwit, although a bit uncommon. In those subjects, take your time to deepen your real understanding. You won't find real, profound understanding in the classroom or in school books. You'll have to add your own research, and often reverse engineer the recipes and rote learning they feed you, to get to the bottom of things. But given that you don't lose time on the crappy subjects (since you aim for mediocre there), you can do it. You'll become an expert in those matters without even noticing it, and for the rest of your life, it'll be a great asset.

Then, concerning the relations with your teachers. Statistically speaking, there will be one in 50 that's actually intelligent and not predominantly concerned with social status and dominance. Ask him or her (and him or her *only*) your difficult questions, preferably in private after the course. (Otherwise, your fellow students won't appreciate you complicating matters in class and will counterattack with even more mockery and bullying than usual.) These rare gems of teachers will appreciate you for your deep interest and will gladly think further together with you.

Concerning all the other teachers, just stay under their radar. Especially don't question their authority in public. Yes, they may be dimwits, yes, they may not have a clue about what they're supposed to be teaching, yes, you may know better than them, yes, it's very tempting to expose all that in public. But bite your tongue and shut up, because when you question their authority, they're forced to retaliate. You have to see it like this: imagine him or her like the alpha chimp in front of a class of young chimps that are all ready to question the alpha's dominant position. If the alpha gives in, it'll ruin his position and life.

Opposing the specific person in power is useless, because even if you succeed in toppling them, their position will be immediately filled by another person. New face, new name, same shit all over. At most the person will change, but the organization won't, and you will have gained nothing. Neurotypicals aren't made for a horizontal social organization. Their social hierarchy, based on Machiavellism, tribalism, deception, and ass-licking is highly bizarre and repulsive to you, but just sweat it out. There's nothing to be gained by entering into the crosshairs of Mr. or Mrs. Alpha. Maintain a low profile as far as these teachers go, don't attract their attention, and you'll be better off.

THE PATRICK BATEMAN PARADOX (NEUROTYPICALS VERSUS PSYCHOPATHS)

> *"I have all the characteristics of a human being: blood, flesh, skin, hair; but not a single, clear, identifiable emotion, except for greed and disgust."*
>
> – Patrick Bateman, the main character in *American Psycho* by Bret Easton Ellis)

A very important distinction to learn to make is between neurotypicals and psychopaths. Why? Because psychopaths camouflage themselves as neurotypicals, but they're not. Psychopaths are dangerous predators or parasites, deranged wolves in neurotypical's clothes, and if you don't learn to recognize them, you're in danger.

Neurotypicals can be annoying if you expect things from them that they're naturally incapable of, but in themselves they're rather innocuous and relatively easy to handle once you know what makes them tick.

Psychopaths, on the other hand, are life-sucking parasites or predators. They'll suck you dry, psychologically, emotionally and financially; engage in relentless revenge for some petty inconvenience you didn't even realize you inadvertently caused them. They'll cold-bloodedly get you out of the way by any means necessary including grave psychological and physical violence, breaking your career, destroying your reputation.

Psycho's make the lives of those around them miserable at the service of their own egotistic needs and desires, and do so well hidden beneath a deceptive cloak of glib friendliness and charm. Psychopaths have very little fear (as opposed to neurotypicals who are quite fearful), are bored as hell because

148

they experience very little emotions, and either don't react at all to other people's pain and suffering, or actively obtain pleasure from it. You can picture them like human-sized praying mantises or spiders.

If you only know psychopaths from Hollywood movies, you definitely need to wise up fast on them because psychopaths are all around you, but the vast majority of them don't even remotely look and behave like the Hollywood cliché. About one in 100 people are estimated to be psychopaths, rising to one in 25 among managers and one in 2 to 3 among prison inmates. That means that in your street there are probably a few; that in your school there are several, both among fellow students and teachers; that in your workplace there are several, especially among the higher functions; and that in your extended family, association, club, or other group you are part of, there are always several operating.

The class bully almost certainly is one. Your funny uncle whose wife is depressed and taking tranquilizers might be one. The neighborhood do-gooder, volunteering to do little chores here and there, may very well be a child-molesting psychopath – or not. They seek out jobs as police officers, judges, managers, and TV personalities, but also as preachers and nurses – anything that gives them power, an aura of morality, and an easy entry into people's personal lives. But you can find them in literally every profession, every form, shape and size, and every social background. They hide in plain sight, playing the friendly and generous typical good neighbor, or even pastor or counselor, whom no-one can imagine being a cold-hearted predator or parasite.

Only a minority of psychopaths are serial killers and/or sexual deviants as portrayed in Hollywood movies. Most stay more or less within the lines of the law, but that doesn't prevent them from completely wrecking countless lives around them. Most of those who *do* get into criminality (white collar or other) are never caught or punished, and succeed perfectly well in passing off as normal or even especially sympathetic people.

Several significant differences between psychopath and non-psychopath brains have been detected in neurobiology, making it clear that psychopathy is certainly not exclusively caused by education or childhood trauma, although these play an important role in how exactly psychopathy manifests itself. It's outside the scope of this book to delve more deeply into psychopathy, but the important point is that since they disguise themselves as neurotypicals, we may be falsely led to believe that a) neurotypicals are meaner and more deceptive than they actually are and b) that several persons in our surroundings are neurotypicals while they're actually psychopaths.

If you don't want to fall prey to psychopaths, you'll have to wise up on them by studying some serious, scientifically backed, non-fiction sources on them. One of the best references is Robert D. Hare, emeritus professor of psychology at the University of British Columbia, and president of Darkstone Research Group, a forensic research and consulting firm. He dedicated his life to the study of psychopaths, and deserves all our attention. You'll be astounded when you start discovering the eye-opening scientific truth about psychopaths, their tremendous impact on everyday life, and the outcomes in the world.

ABOUT THE AUTHOR

Abel Abelson, an intellectually gifted neurodivergent, was probably left on this planet by an alien race that forgot to pick him up again. While waiting for their return, Abel turns his stay on Earth to good use (and has good fun in the process) by doing zoological research and reconnaissance missions, and reporting the results in his books.

Setting free the intellectually gifted: Diary of an extra-terrestrial Earthling

At forty years of age, Abel Abelson discovers that he is intellectually gifted. Suddenly his eternal "otherness" is no longer a flaw. It is being called an asset, a plus, a gift ... But is it really?

In the light of this discovery Abel revisits his past, unravels the present and reconstructs a future. Being intellectually gifted is just the tip of the iceberg. True meaning turns out to be hiding somewhere else, far beyond the "giftedness" concept.

Open, direct and compelling - Abel's diary speaks of love, failed over and over again, but finally won; of emancipation in a confused and confusing world; of emotions, profound and overwhelming; of ideas, old and new; of feeling different; of being lost, then found.

Meet Abel: man, simian, human being, lover, hater, son, father, husband, hermit, child, adult, loser, finder. Above all: someone like you. Or not.

ISBN-13: 978-1530637133

I, the fly

I think, therefore I am a fly on an elephant's head.

I, the fly, commands a huge elephant, all by herself. Or is that just what she is thinking? And what adventures do they live together?

A good-humored story for children of all ages, with a twist or two and a surprising, funny end.

A parable about arrogance, friendship, missed opportunities and what really matters in life. And for those willing: an original reflection on consciousness and (the absence of) free will.

ISBN-13: 978-1532791376

1   "You can clearly see how quickly the brain decides when you
     meet new people. In collaboration with the American speed
     dating service HurryDate, psychologist Robert Kurzban
     conducted an experiment with 10,000 people.
     Each person met 25 potential partners in one evening and had
     three minutes to form an impression.
     But the study found that after just three seconds on average,
     people are already sure whether they find someone attractive or
     not.
     Psychologist Alexander Todorov came to a similar conclusion.
     He had 245 subjects look at photos of different faces for 0.1
     seconds, 0.5 seconds, 1 second, or indefinitely, and then asked
     subjects to rate the faces. The conclusion was that after only 0.1
     seconds they had already judged how confident, competent,
     comfortable, aggressive or attractive the people in the photos
     were. And if the subjects were given longer time to look at the
     faces, they did not change their views."
     (Logisch denken zit er niet in, Gorm Palmgren, Wetenschap in
     Beeld, https://wibnet.nl/mens/hersenen/logisch-denken-zit-er-
     niet-in, 2020)

2   Turnbaugh, P. J., Ley, R. E., Hamady, M., Fraser-Liggett, C. M.,
     Knight, R., & Gordon, J. I. (2007). The human microbiome
     project. Nature, 449(7164), 804-810.

3   Cfr. the interesting case of Jack Yufe and Oskar Stöhr, identical
     twins separated shortly after birth. At 21 years of age they found
     each other. Both flushed the toilet before and after using it, both
     read the endings of books first, both wrapped tape around pens
     and pencils to get a better grip, and both enjoyed dipping
     buttered toast in their coffee.

4   Cambridge dictionary, definition B1 of "society *noun*
     (PEOPLE)",
     https://dictionary.cambridge.org/dictionary/english/society,
     retrieved July 20th, 2020

5   The durian seems to be the perfect fruity metaphor for a
     neurodivergent. "The durian is spiky all over (...). Its shape is
     irregular. Even its weight is not standard. (...) Just as the shape

and size can vary, the color of the outer shell can range from green to light brown. The texture of the fruit's flesh can vary from dry and rough to smooth and moist. The color of the flesh can range from whitish to yellowish to reddish. And perhaps most fascinatingly of all, the flavor can actually vary from one durian to another. (...) If you are new to the durian (...), your first encounter might send you to hell, as it will smell and taste simply awful. But if you persist, you may find yourself coming to appreciate the truly sublime nature of this fantastic fruit." (The World's Weirdest and Most Exotic Fruits, Justin Choo, Delishably, https://delishably.com/fruits/Worlds-Weirdest-Fruits, updated on February 6, 2020)

6   "Consider the humble slime mold. (...) [W]hen they are threatened by starvation, the tiny amoebae coalesce into slug-like creatures that then aggregate into a large, swaying tower that grows upward with a burgeoning slimy top—until that top sticks to an unwitting passing insect, the starvation-resistant spores hitchhiking out into the world, while all the individuals making up the base and stalk die." Evolution selects for 'loners' that hang back from collective behavior—at least in slime molds, by Princeton University, Phys.org, March 19, 2020, https://phys.org/news/2020-03-evolution-loners-behaviorat-slime-molds.html)

7   Waal, Frans de; Waal, Frans B. M. (2007-09-30). Chimpanzee Politics: Power and Sex Among Apes. JHU Press. ISBN 9780801886560.

8   "This book [...] demonstrates something we had already suspected on the grounds of the close connection between apes and man: that the social organization of chimpanzees is almost too human to be true." (Frans de Waal, Chimpanzee Politics: Power and Sex Among Apes)

9   "Tsze-Kung asked, saying, 'Is there one word which may serve as a rule of practice for all one's life?' The Master said, 'Is not Reciprocity such a word? What you do not want done to yourself, do not do to others.' (Confucius, Analects, http://classics.mit.edu/Confucius/analects.mb.txt)

10   See for instance the work of Robert B. Cialdini, Ph.D., and more specifically his book "Influence: The Psychology of Persuasion" (2006), where reciprocity is presented as one of the six fundamental "weapons" of persuasion. Cialdini also nothes that anthropologist Richard Leakey considers the rule of reciprocity as a defining factor of what it means to be human,:"We are human because our ancestors learned to share their food and their skills in an honored network of obligation".

11   Cialdini, Robert B., Ph.D., 2006). Influence: The Psychology of Persuasion. Harper Business. ISBN 978-0061241895.

12   I use the word 'animal' here in a biological sense, not in a depreciative manner. We neurodivergents are just as primal and animalistic as neurotypicals are. We're all animals under the sun, all of equal value, it's only that neurotypicals and neurodivergents are different types of animals, which is crucial to understand if we're going to live more harmoniously on the same planet.

13   See among others "Chimpanzee Politics: Power and Sex Among Apes" by Frans de Waal for many examples of quite sophisticated deceptions among chimps.

Printed in Dunstable, United Kingdom